Illustrated

TRIUMPH
MOTORCYCLES
BUYER'S ★ GUIDE™

Third Edition

From 1945 Through the Latest Models

Roy Bacon

Niton Publishing

This third edition published in 1997 by Niton Publishing, PO Box 3, Ventnor, Isle of Wight P038 2BE England

The information in this book is true and complete to the best of our knowledge. All recommendations are made without any guarantee on the part of the author or publisher, who also disclaim any liability incurred in connection with the use of this data or specific details

We recognize that some words, model names and designations, for example, mentioned herein are the property of the trademark holder. We use them for identification purposes only. This is not an official publication

British Library Cataloguing in Publication Data
A catalogue record for this book is available from the British Library
ISBN 1 85579 033 5

On the front cover: At the front stands a 1969 Bonneville from the Meriden past, restored by Steve Hamel and owned by Wendy, that is still the leader in the classic bike field; behind is a 1996 1200 Daytona from the range now produced at Hinckley to represent today, compliments of Metropolitan Honda–Yamaha–Triumph–Ducati, St. Paul, Minnesota. *Tim Remus*

On the back cover: First of a long line, the 1938 Speed Twin 500 cc; nearing the end of a long line, the 1972 five-speed Trident triple.

Printed and bound in the United States of America

Contents

Acknowledgments

A decade ago Tim Parker recruited me to write for Osprey, and changed my life. His support when I first gave up my job, and later moved house, helped over the difficult times, and together we produced a series of motorcycle titles the reading public seemed to approve of.

Tim moved on to Motorbooks International in America, and we were soon talking of a new motorcycle series. From that came this volume, and another first for myself with my own imprint. Suddenly, all those publisher decisions about spending money meant something, but they were taken and I hope you like the result.

Tim acted as the catalyst that caused the book to be written but I am equally in the debt of ace restorer Hughie Hancox who took time out from his busy life restoring Triumphs to read the manuscript for me. His comments and additions helped greatly to round out a number of points.

For the pictures I turned once more to the magazines and have to thank Malcolm Gough, editor of *Motor Cycle News*, and EMAP, whose archives hold the old *Motor Cycle Weekly* files. Others came from Ivor Davies, for many years publicity manager at Triumph, and the Vintage Motor Cycle Club courtesy of Frank Webber, photo librarian. A number of the pictures I took myself, mainly at shows or museums, as will be clear from their background.

Some of the photographs carry the imprint of professionals and these came from Richard Bailey, Brian Holder, Nick Nicholls and Don Page.

Finally, my thanks to the professionals of the printing and book binding industry who helped me bring my first imprint to completion.

Roy Bacon
Niton
Isle of Wight
February 1989

For this second edition I have added a chapter to cover the new Hinckley multis produced by John Bloor's team and on the market from 1991. They continue the Triumph story in a new format and every indication is that they will succeed.

At the same time some extra data on US models has been added, this having come to hand in recent times. These machines were never seen in their home country and nothing on them would be published in the press of the day. Now we know a little more so can expand the story. Always, there seem to be extra things that come to light over the years so there are a few corrections and some more pages so we could include some material that was squeezed out first time round.

My thanks to Hinckley for checking the material in that chapter, press photographs and the VIN numbers. My thanks to several American correspondents who have sent me additional data on Triumph US versions over the years and to British ditto for other extra material.

For this third edition the Hinckley data has been extended to 1997 to bring the story up to date. No doubt it will need further extension as they introduce new models.

Roy Bacon
November 1996

Introduction

This buyer's guide covers postwar and some prewar Triumph motorcycles, so is mainly concerned with the twins but does not ignore the Cub or Trident models. It takes in the prewar Turner and Val Page twins, the singles from 1936 and the postwar scooters. The German Triumph-Werke Nurnberg, or TWN, is not included as the connection with the English firm ceased in 1929.

The Triumph Twin was one of the most popular models on the market from 1945 on, and the interest in the marque has continued with the classic revival of the 1980s. Because of this there are many machines still run-

Graham Walker, long time-editor of *Motor Cycling* and TT winner, on the 1938 Speed Twin which began the famous Triumph twin line. Edward Turner, who ran the firm for so long, stands beside the 1959 unit construction version which replaced it. Still in the same Amaranth Red colour and concept, but with different details and retaining the typical Triumph lines.

Brilliant development engineer Doug Hele, left, with Bert Hopwood who was responsible for many postwar British designs. Here they inspect a 1972 650 twin which has a lower seat than the first 1971 oil-in-frame model. It was their clever work that dealt with that crisis—but there were more to come.

ning and being bought or sold, but not all are what they may pretend to be. It is all too easy to switch parts to build a machine that may, on the surface, appear correct. This book will help you make sure it is, as far as one can judge from an external examination.

Engine and frame numbers, the identity charts in the appendices and as much information as possible are your weapons when buying, and with them hopefully you can find what you are looking for. There is more on this in the last chapter, but first we will go on a Triumph model tour to see what was on offer and when.

Each chapter covers a specific section of the Triumph range and includes an investment rating using stars from one to five.

Remember that they are at best an educated guess based on conditions in 1988 and could be entirely wrong. Thus there is no guarantee given or implied and we can all have a good laugh about them in 1998.

Always check out current prices in your part of the world before buying, for these can be greatly affected by events. Few of us realized how the market would change during the 1980s, and over the next decade it could alter as much again in either direction.

Investment ratings

Here is how the star system works:
★★★★★ Five-star models are the tops, command the highest prices and usually have the best chance of appreciating. They

The Trident in its Hurricane form and Craig Vetter styling. The three exhaust systems on the right were most distinctive as was the fibreglass bodywork. The forks were extended a little in chopper style to lengthen the wheelbase and the bars stood high and handsome.

are most likely to be sold by contacts and word of mouth, sometimes at auctions or more expensively by a specialist dealer.

★★★★ Four-stars are the best that most people can hope to find, as there are not enough five-star machines to go round. Still, very desirable and worth having from all points of view. If advertised, check carefully, as a poor one will cost to get into true four-star condition.

★★★ Three-stars are middle-of-the-road, nice machines that hold their price along with market trends. Most machines in daily use come from this class, where good condition and reliability are the norm but must be checked for.

★★ Two-stars are the least liked, least able to keep up their value with the market but can still be nice machines if they are what you want.

★ One-stars are the type few want, are nonoriginal or need too much work to be correct. A one-star can be a long shot, although this is unlikely now, but as always,

if it is the bike you want you can probably get it fairly cheap.

Along with the investment rating, one must consider the three C's—complete, correct and condition. All have a major effect on the price of the machine but not its ultimate star rating. Being complete is important on a machine bought for restoration, and it is the small details that matter more than the large.

There are many small items in the build-up of a machine and finding all the missing ones can be expensive and time consuming. Correct parts are just as important for restoration, although less so for a machine for daily use. The reverse applies to condition, for the restorer is mainly concerned with having correct parts regardless, more or less, of their condition, while the daily rider wants top condition whether the part is correct or a modern equivalent.

As always, you make your decision and pay your money. Whatever your choice, I hope it brings you good riding and much enjoyment, which just might be better than buying that five-star investment you dare not take out on the road.

This is the Thunderbird that was introduced for 1995 as a classic roadster and proved a great success with its features from the past, here in the 1997 livery.

The 1200 Trophy as it was revised for 1996, complete with new fairing shape, twin headlamps and panniers; this a 1997 model.

Chapter 1

Pre-unit twins

★★★★	6/1 1934-36
★★★★★	6/1 plus sidecar 1934-36
★★	3T 1946-51
★★★★	5T Speed Twin 1938-39
★★★	5T Speed Twin 1946-58
★★★	6T Thunderbird 1950-62
★★★★★	T100 Tiger 100 1939
★★★★	T100 Tiger 100 1946-59
★★★	T110 Tiger 110 1954-55
★★★★	T110 Tiger 110 1956-59
★★★	T110 Tiger 110 1960-61
★★★★★	T120 Bonneville 1959
★★★★	T120 Bonneville 1960-62
★★★★★	TR5 Trophy 1949-50
★★★★	TR5 Trophy 1951-54
★★★	TR5 Trophy 1955-58
★★★★	TR6 Trophy 1956-60
★★★	TR6 Trophy 1961-62

The definitive Triumph twin has to be that designed by Edward Turner, but this was not the first such engine built by the firm. There had been a prototype back in 1913, following earlier trials with a Bercley in 1909, and some twenty years later came their first production twin.

This was designed by Val Page, more for sidecar use than as a solo, and was not to remain long in the model range. Once Turner was in the saddle at Triumph, he soon made his mark on the way the firm was run and on its products, with first the single-cylinder Tiger range and then his own Speed Twin.

Page twin

The Page twin was a solid job, both in appearance and construction, and was an-

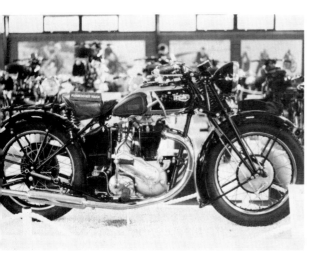

Before the famous Edward Turner twin, Triumph built one of 646 cc designed by Val Page. This was essentially a sidecar machine and the engine and frame reflected this, although the machine could be used solo. This is a restored example from 1934 when it still had hand change for the four gears.

The drive side of the 646 cc Page twin. The engine had a gear-driven single camshaft located behind the one-piece block and separate cylinder heads. The primary drive was by expensive double helical gears, but the gearbox was conventional English. The model was soon replaced by the Turner twin.

First of a long line was the 1938 Speed Twin with that well-known style to both engine and machine. The original six studs holding the block down proved marginal and became eight the next year. There was no surround for the front number plate as yet.

nounced in July 1933. It had a vertical twin engine of 646 cc with overhead valves and gear primary drive to its four-speed gearbox. This unit was installed in conventional cycle parts. With it was offered a new sidecar specially designed to match it, which had an enveloping body to conceal the main chassis.

The engine had a number of unusual features, although in the main it followed accepted practice. The crankcase split on its vertical centre line; inside it the crankshaft, forged as one with three bob-weights, ran on ball races. The case extended down to form an oil tank for the dry-sump system and had a mounting face at the rear for the gearbox.

A one-piece iron block sat on the case with a tunnel cast in at the rear for the pushrods, but the cylinder heads were separate although also in iron. The rocker supports bolted on top with a split, two-piece alloy cover to enclose the rockers, except for their outer ends. The camshaft was sited high up in the crankcase behind the block where it was driven by a train of gears that continued on to the rear-mounted mag-dyno. It ran in

ball races, and in addition to the four cams, above which sat the tappets in their housing, it had an eccentric next to them to operate the oil pump.

The internal bob-weights were supplemented by a flywheel fitted between the left-side main bearing and the output drive which incorporated a ramp-type shock absorber. The four-speed, hand-change gearbox bolted to the rear of the crankcase and was driven by a double helical gear pair, which must have been expensive to make and install correctly.

The chaincase was in alloy with the inner cast as part of the crankcase and the outer held by a run of small screws. The clutch was a normal multi-plate type and the gearbox was equally conventional English, so the final-drive sprocket was inboard of the clutch and the top gear ratio unit. Due to all of this the engine rotated in the reverse direction to normal, which no doubt caught a few owners by surprise over the years.

The whole unit went into a massive, rigid duplex cradle frame fitted with heavy-duty girder forks at the front, but solo ground clearance was limited due to the intended sidecar use. Both wheels had offset hubs with 8 in. single-leading shoe brakes, and these were interconnected with a parking mechanism.

The remainder of the machine was built along the same lines with massive mudguards, large saddle, rear carrier, and instrument panel set in the petrol tank. Although the oil was carried in the dry sump, there appeared to be a tank under the saddle in the usual place, but this was a pressure filter housing piped into the system.

The sidecar that went with this twin had a special chassis with the bodywork designed to conceal it. It was a single-seater with fold-down hood and attached to the machine at four points. The body was suspended on elliptic springs at front and rear and the mudguard was faired into it, a feature that was not at all common in that era.

The machine was not a great sales success even though the firm won the prestigious Maudes Trophy with it. This was given for the best standard machine exploit of the year, and was an important contest in the period between World Wars I and II. To earn the award the 6/1, as the machine was listed, covered 500 miles at Brooklands in 500 minutes, running with the sidecar, and prior to this had been taken through the 1933 International Six Days Trial (ISDT).

Despite this feat it did not attract many buyers, for it was expensive and not too well suited to solo use. For the sidecar rider it fell between two stools, as those with the money bought a big vee-twin and those without had to stick with a single. There were virtually no modifications during the model's short life, although a foot gearchange became an option. The Page twin was dropped from the range at the end of the 1936 season.

Prospects

The Page twin has to be four stars going on five, for it is now a rare model. Because it falls in the post-vintage era and lacks the light charm of the later twins, it fails to get that final star but comes close.

With the correct, period sidecar it would have to make five stars, for such an outfit would be extremely rare and one of the best investments.

Turner twins

The Triumph Speed Twin was announced to the public in *The Motor Cycle* dated July 29, 1937, and straight away set a new style for the rest of the industry to follow. With the

After the war, Triumph introduced the 349 cc 3T based on a wartime model as far as the engine internals went. Thus, the crankshaft differs from the rest as does the head with integral rocker box. The frame was lighter than the others but the forks, wheels and details were mainly common. A nice machine of the time and here in 1948 form.

The famous Triumph nacelle was introduced for 1949 and is here seen on a 5T. At the same time the instruments moved into its top face, so the tank panel was soon replaced by a parcel grid. Not all riders liked the sprung rear hub fitted here, but the machine itself was popular.

advent of the war two years later, it was some ten years or more before other firms could introduce their version of the vertical twin, and few caught up.

The Speed Twin was designed by Edward Turner, who moved to Triumph in 1936 as chief designer and general manager, and who stayed there for the rest of his working life except for a brief wartime period. He was an autocratic man with a hot temper, and ran Triumph efficiently by driving a small management team hard. They were expected to achieve the impossible and usually did, although often under considerable stress.

The 499 cc Speed Twin set a style that the Triumph twin used to the end of its days, and benefited from two Turner design characteristics. The first was to make things small, light and simple, which has to be done at the design stage. It is never feasible to add such characteristics later. The result can then be tested and only the items that prove inadequate need to be strengthened, so the result is close to the optimum.

The machine that comes from this process will always operate in an eager manner and boast good performance. To this, Turner added something even more important which was his flair for style and his judgement as to what the public would accept and buy. He had an uncanny knack of getting it just right in these two vital areas which played a great part in the marque's success for so long.

When introduced, the Speed Twin looked much like a twin-port single, at a time when that style was popular, even if expensive in exhaust systems. The engine was compact and so fitted into the standard single-cylinder cycle parts. The resulting machine weighed less than the equivalent single and only cost £5 more.

The engine was no more complex than a single. It was based on a 360 degree crankshaft with its even firing interval, as any other arrangement would have precluded the use of a single carburettor and the basic twin-cylinder magneto. All subsequent twins

The Thunderbird joined the Triumph range for 1950 and was introduced with a 500 mile high-speed run by three models at Montlhery near Paris. It also came with the new four-bar tank badge, revised tank finish with no chrome plating and the parcel grid. The saddle is here replaced by the optional twin seat.

that went into production were to keep to the original layout even when unit construction was added.

The bottom half was a vertically split alloy crankcase in which the built up crankshaft ran in two good-sized ball races. The crankshaft comprised two stampings, one for each cylinder, which bolted to a central flywheel with spigots for location. The connecting rods were in light alloy and ran directly on the crankpins with steel caps lined with white metal. Bronze small end bushes were used.

The right end of the crankshaft carried a gear which meshed with an intermediate and this in turn drove the two camshafts. These were ahead of and behind the cylinder line and were as high as was practical in the crankcase. Each had two cams near its centre which lifted tappets in a housing set in the cylinder block.

A one-piece cast-iron block was used and was held to the crankcase by six studs and nuts for that first year. In it ran flat-topped pistons with three rings and on top of it went a one-piece cylinder head, also in cast iron. The valves were set out at ninety degrees, the classic figure for the time, suiting the piston shape and compression ratio. In later years it was to inhibit performance.

Two separate alloy boxes carried the rockers on fixed spindles with caps to give access to the valve adjusters in the outer rocker ends. Pushrods connected the rockers to the tappet movement and were encased in smart chrome-plated tubes fore and aft of the block. The Triumph factory and thousands of twin owners were to spend the next half century trying to keep the oil inside those tubes!

The oil was supplied by a dry sump system with external tank and used a twin plunger pump for supply and return. It was sited in the timing chest where it was driven from the inlet camshaft gear nut and supplied, via a pressure release valve, to the crankshaft. An external line fed the rocker gear with a takeoff to a tank-mounted pressure gauge. Oil from the valve wells drained via external pipes to the pushrod tubes and then down to the sump. A diaphragm breather went in the drive-side crankcase wall.

The electrics were a Lucas mag-dyno mounted behind the cylinder block on a platform formed in the crankcase casting. It was gear driven from the inlet camshaft gear so was yet another feature that continued the single cylinder appearance so necessary to sell to the conservative motorcycle buyer. Another was the Type 6 Amal carburettor fitted to an alloy manifold bolted to the head. On the exhaust side there was a separate pipe and low level silencer on each side with a nice clean line to it.

The engine fitted into the same set of cycle parts as used by the sporting Tiger 90 single and other 500 cc models with virtually no change. It drove a four-speed gearbox with footchange by a single strand chain with a smart alloy primary chaincase. This had a streamlined bulge at the front to enclose the engine shock absorber and a single cap to pour oil into and give access for chain tension checks. The two case halves were held together by a row of small screws and the assembly gave a nice line to the left side of the machine for many a year.

The Speed Twin became the standard machine for the London Metropolitan police after the war and for many other police forces all over the world. These are Speed Twins of the early fifties on duty in 1959, with Prime Minister Macmillan and President Eisenhower at London Airport.

This is a 1958 Speed Twin being checked over. By then the model had a pivoted fork frame and new tank badge but retained the nacelle for the front forks. The engine had gained an alternator and coil ignition, with the points in place of the magneto and none too accessible for servicing.

The clutch was as on the other models. The external clutch lever was typical Triumph in style and from 1939 had a small rubber cover over the end where the cable attached. The gearbox was typical English with both gear and kickstart pedals on the right and included an external pointer and scale to show the gear engaged.

The gearbox moved to adjust the primary chain and it and the engine went into a built-up cradle frame, rigid at the rear, with girder front forks. The wheel sizes differed with a 3.00x20 in. tyre at the front and 3.50x19 in. at the rear, but both hubs were offset and contained single-leading-shoe brakes working in 7 in. drums. The front one drove the speedometer which was mounted on top of the girder fork and thus had a hard ride.

The remainder of the cycle parts were quite conventional so there was a saddle and a rear stand. The dynamo control box went under the seat and in the same area the oil tank went on the right and the battery on the left. A toolbox fitted in the angle of the right chainstays and was triangular in shape.

The petrol tank had a top panel set in it to carry the ammeter, oil pressure gauge, light switch and an inspection lamp. Finish of the machine was in the famous Amaranth Red while the tank and wheel rims were chrome

This 1958 Thunderbird shared most of its cycle parts with the rest of the range, but kept to its SU carburettor. It had an all-iron engine, although the alloy head was by then in use on the T110, and rather weak pivoted fork frame.

plated. The first had gold-lined, red panels and the second the same treatment for the rim centres while the mudguards were also gold lined. The headlamp shell was chrome plated and the overall effect was truly dramatic.

Thus began the Triumph twin line and the Speed Twin was an instant success. It looked right, it performed well, it made the right noises and it was at the right price. Essentially the design was right for, aside from the engine, it comprised tried and tested parts and the engine too had few real faults. The only one of note in the early days lay in the six-stud block fixing and for 1939 this was altered to give a thicker block flange and eight studs.

From then on the twins developed, but all can be seen to come from the original.

Touring twins

The touring twins were the 3T, 5T and 6T of 349, 499 and 649 cc. By definition, these were the most docile of the model range. They were the machines bought for riding to work, weekend runs and touring although in truth, the 6T was first introduced to answer the call from America for more cubic inches. In time its role as top performer was taken over by more sporting machines.

The 5T or Speed Twin, was the first of the line and changed little for 1939 on the surface. In fact the alteration from six to eight barrel studs meant fairly major alterations to the casting patterns and new parts for crankcase and block. Otherwise the changes were minimal and amounted to a chromed surround for the front number plate and a rear chain oiler. This drew its supply from the primary chaincase and was controlled by a needle valve. It was an arrangement which was to remain a Triumph feature on all pre-unit models.

Before the war ended Triumph had made their plans for the future and announced their postwar range in March 1945. Its basis remained the Speed Twin, but alongside it was the smaller and lighter 3T which was always to be simply known by this designation.

The 5T was much the same as before in nearly all respects but did incorporate two

Harry Louis, *Motor Cycle* editor, and Neale Shilton, Triumph sales manager, see Vic Willoughby, also of *Motor Cycle*, off on a 1960 Thunderbird from the Triumph works. It was the first year for the duplex frame, which had to be quickly stiffened after early failures, and for the bathtub on this model.

noticeable changes. The first was the addition of telescopic front forks in place of the older girders, and with them a reduction of headlamp size to 7 in. The second was the separation of the mag-dyno into its two parts with the magneto flange mounted to the rear of the engine, much as before. Its driving gear included an automatic advance mechanism so the magneto itself had fixed internal timing for an optimum spark.

The dynamo was moved to the front of the crankcase which was amended so it could be clamped in place with a securing band. The drive was by a pinion which meshed with the exhaust camshaft gear via a hole in the back of the timing chest wall. Less obvious changes were to a speedometer drive from the rear wheel, to 19 in. diameter for the front and to the rocker feed and drain oil lines. The feed was taken from the main return line and thus was no longer at pump pressure, while the drain was via internal drillings, so the small external pipes dis-

For the police, the Thunderbird was fitted with magneto ignition to help the alternator cope with the extra electrical equipment fitted. Some versions had a dynamo as well, and the specification varied to suit the force. This one is from 1960.

This is the final form of the pre-unit Thunderbird in 1962 when it had a siamesed exhaust system. It retained the bathtub and many other features from the past, while the full-width front hub and alloy head date from the year before.

appeared. Even less obvious was a change to the engine breather which became a timed disc driven by the inlet camshaft. This replaced the prewar design.

The Speed Twin suited its times well, for it allied performance with style and comfort. First gear always went in with a crunch at the start of a ride, but the gearchange was fine for the rest of the time. Handling and brakes were acceptable and the whole added up to a desirable machine.

The 3T was more than just a 5T with a smaller engine, and was to remain the odd one of the twins for its short production life. While there were many common parts, especially details, a good number of major items differed. Because it was smaller it never rated the regard given the Speed Twin, but its smoothly delivered, even if limited, power gave it a charm to those whose riding style matched it.

The 3T engine had a reduced bore and stroke compared with the Speed Twin, and internally was altered a good deal. This began with the crankshaft which was still built up but in a manner that allowed the use of one-piece steel connecting rods. This was done by forging each outer web, mainshaft and crankpin as one part with the pin clamped into a central flywheel. It was to prove adequate for the limited power involved. The assembly turned in a bush on the timing side while retaining a ball race for the drive.

The top half differed from the larger model in having the rocker boxes cast as part of the iron cylinder head. Long through studs with top bolts held down head and block unlike the 5T, so all the major engine parts were different. The timing gear, oil pump and electrics remained the same.

Apart from the engine changes the frame was lighter and a good number of the cycle parts differed from those of the 5T. The gearbox remained the same, as did most of the clutch and the wheels, but not the primary chaincase or the exhaust pipes or

Postwar, the Tiger 100 continued to be a sports version of the Speed Twin with its own finish and style. Much was common and thus this 1949 example still had an iron engine and saddle plus pillion seat, but had gained the nacelle and parcel grid. A charming and fast machine on the road.

silencers. The overall result was a machine that was a little awkward to produce with the other twins and which had a somewhat select market.

These two models progressed into 1947 with the option of rear suspension. This was the famous, or infamous, sprung hub which could be switched for the normal wheel and had a limited movement. The springs and all

The Tiger 100 was introduced for 1939 with a mildly tuned 5T engine fitted into common cycle parts. The finish was bright, as for the other Tiger models, and an inspired styling feature was the lovely megaphone silencers, each with a detachable end.

the other parts, including curved sliders that kept the wheel moving in an arc about the gearbox sprocket, were contained within the full-width hub. Do not even think of opening the spring boxes without the right equipment, as this is very dangerous. The ride it gave could be equally exciting and many owners came to prefer the predictable rigid frame to the hub and the weave it could set up.

Where the sprung hub was fitted it was no longer possible to drive the speedometer from the rear wheel, so this was taken from the gearbox. Around the same time, both close- and wide-ratio gear sets became available and may be found in any machine.

A detail change to the electrics was to a domed glass for the headlamp in place of the earlier flat type, while an odd distinction affected the spark plugs. For 1946 all models were listed with Lodge plugs, but for 1947 these only went in the 5T while the 3T had Champions—if you believe the parts list.

The 5T was virtually unaltered for 1948, but during the year the 3T engine was modi-fied to delete the long through studs for head and block. In their place went the Speed Twin type with short studs for the block and bolts for the head.

That was the last engine change for the 3T, but both models had improved cycle parts for 1949. The machine styling was altered by the appearance of the Triumph nacelle on the top of the front forks. This was well shaped and carried light unit, switches and instruments in one to clean up the lines.

With the nacelle there was no need for the instrument panel in the tank, so that was replaced by a plated parcel grid which was fitted and proved popular. To replace the oil gauge, a telltale was added to the pressure release valve which was easier to make and stopped riders from worrying about the lubrication system.

There was another model and a good few changes for 1950 to start Triumph off well for the decade. New was the 6T which was given the name Thunderbird, and obtained its 649 cc from a larger bore and a stroke two

For 1951 the T100 engine changed to the close-pitched fin, light-alloy top half. With the four-bar tank badge adopted the year before, this gave it altered looks while keeping the Triumph line. The model came as standard with the twin seat which suited it.

millimetres up from that of the 5T. In most respects it was much like the Speed Twin with minor internal differences. A feature, shared by both but not the 3T, was the reappearance of the external drain pipes from the valve wells to the pushrod covers.

Due to the added power of the 6T it was necessary to uprate the gearbox, and Triumph took the opportunity to improve the design in various ways. The speedometer drive became part of the box rather than something tacked on as an afterthought, and the internals were improved. The new box went on all models and the alternative ratios continued to be options.

The Thunderbird put a real edge on Triumph twin performance and strained the sprung hub even more. With its crisp gear change the machine would out-accelerate most other vehicles on the road, but if the road curved then so did the path of the twin as soon as 65 mph or so came up on the dial. If the curve and the open throttle continued, the machine would keep up its weave as the rider went on up through the gears and approached 90 mph. The problem seldom became worse and in time owners got used

to it, but it was disconcerting the first time round.

The 1950 model range was given a new look by a change to the fuel tank styling. In place of the chrome plating and lined panels, the tanks were simply painted and then fitted with styling bands on each side. These comprised four horizontal lines with the Triumph name included in them, and the design saved on the use of nickel which was in short supply at the time.

Among the details there was a change to a longer dynamo with greater output, a better control unit for it and a revised sprung hub. A twin seat appeared on the options list to replace the normal saddle, but was not available for the 3T due to its different frame.

Having introduced a new model and revised the others, Triumph took a rest for 1951 and just changed the filler cap to a bayonet type. At the end of the year the 3T was dropped. It was the least profitable to make, its production differed from the

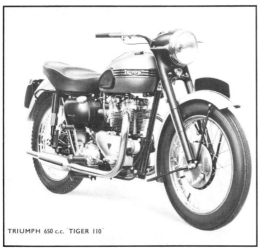

TRIUMPH 650 c.c. 'TIGER 110'

The Tiger 110 with 649 cc engine was introduced in 1954 with the pivoted fork frame. From the start it had the 8 in. front brake with air scoop, but for 1956 it was fitted with an alloy head as seen here. Rather a fast engine for the frame.

This is the 1957 Tiger 110 on show at Earls Court with its new grill tank badge but otherwise much as before. The machine behind it is the streamlined record breaker with 650 Triumph engine, which the world knew did 214 mph in 1956 although this was never ratified by the FIM.

The final pre-unit Tiger 100 was built in 1959 and had some internal engine changes. On the outside it was much as before but did have a full-width front brake from the year before. A fine and fast motorcycle, although the speed was really ahead of the handling.

others significantly and the firm could sell everything it could build anyway.

The only model to receive an easily noticed change for 1952 was the 6T which was fitted with an SU carburettor in place of the usual Amal. To get it in, the frame seat tube had to have a lug inserted into it for the air hose. This alteration went on the 5T as well. The other noted change was to an underslung pilot lamp of rectangular form which went

This is the Tiger 110 from the 1958-59 period, when much of it was common with other models of the range. A two-tone tank finish was available which set the lines off nicely, and it continued to be one of the most popular machines on the market.

beneath the headlamp, while the petrol tank design was altered so it had a central seam running along its top.

It was the 5T's turn for changes in 1953 when it was fitted with a Lucas alternator on the left side of the engine in the primary chaincase. To suit this, the transmission shock absorber was moved into the clutch for all models and a distributor replaced the magneto on the 5T. For this model alone, the dynamo was removed and coil ignition with emergency start added, while all machines were fitted with a rectangular rear lamp.

The 6T received the alternator plus coil ignition and distributor in 1954, and at the same time its timing-side main bearing was increased in size and the crankcase with it to suit. This case had an extra bulge under the timing chest and is quite easy to distinguish from the older type. The 5T was given the larger main bearing and associated crank-case for 1955, when it also changed to a Monobloc carburettor. That year the major change to both models was to a pivoted fork frame. They were also both fitted with a dual seat as standard, a rear lamp with built-in reflector and a rear brake torque stay.

The new frame did not help the handling much, for the subframe only bolted to the main one and the rear fork was none too well supported either. Replacement of its bushes was to be one of the worst of Triumph jobs. The spindle was a press fit in the frame and had to come out to release the fork. It would either refuse to budge or seize in its bushes, turn in the frame and wear this away. Either event made the task a difficult one.

The unpopular underslung pilot lamp was replaced in 1956 by a horn grill, while the parcel grid was amended from five longitudinal bars to four. This suited the centre tank seam which was given a chrome-plated band.

The tank badge changed for 1957 to a grill form, while the front forks had the wheel mountings altered to split clamps. Both models were fitted with new full-width front hubs although the brake size stayed at 7 in.

The gearbox was amended for 1958 to provide the Slickshift clutch operation, where the clutch was raised by the movement of the gear pedal. To suit it, the gearbox end cover was modified, but it was far from a popular innovation and it is common to find that the operating roller has been removed at some time. The device tended to spoil the gearchange and if the rider pressed the pedal to make sure of engagement, the clutch was lifted again which was disconcerting. A steering lock was also added that year, the final year for the Speed Twin, which left the 6T the sole pre-unit tourer.

It continued in 1959 with a change to a Monobloc carburettor in place of the SU and

The nacelle fitted only on the Bonneville T120 for its first 1959 year, when it was really a T110 plus twin-carburettor option and had just made it into the sales brochure. It went on to become a legend and one of the most popular twins of all time, and is here seen in the livery used for the latter part of that first year.

The 1961 T110, which had changed a good deal from the original sports form. In this, its final year, it had the duplex frame common to the 649 cc models, the bathtub from the tourers and an alternator although at least the magneto was still in place.

the next year went into a new, duplex frame. The early versions of this had their problems but the quick addition of a bracing tube under the top tube solved these. The model was also fitted with the Triumph bathtub that year, this being the rear enclosure first seen on a unit construction model in 1957. It enclosed the rear part of the machine but not the rear wheel, and was topped by a hinged seat.

For 1961 the Thunderbird was finally given an alloy head and with this the external oil drains were dispensed with. To go with the added performance from the new head there was an 8 in. front brake still in a full-width hub. The model had only one more year to run in pre-unit form, and for 1962 lost the Slickshift and gained a sia-mesed exhaust system. At the end of that season the original 1937 design came to an end as well, after a quarter of a century's service.

Prospects
For the Speed Twin and Thunderbird, the frame type plays a major part in a buyer's choice of model but is unlikely to have too much effect on the way they appreciate. They were middle-of-the road machines and so rate three stars each.

Older models, especially the 1950-54 6T, could manage four stars as the top of the line in their day, and the prewar 5T certainly warrants four stars. A really nice early 5T with six-stud block could make five stars and must be a good investment.

The 3T is down to two stars, although it is a charming motorcycle to own. It is just that not too many people know it exists. Much of the machine differs from the Triumph main-stream and buyers prefer the larger engines. If you want one anyway, don't expect its value to do more than keep one step behind the market.

Sports twins
The sports twins are the Tiger models that inherited the brilliant name first used for the sporting singles in 1936. This was one of Edward Turner's most astute moves, for he added chrome and style to some prosaic models and gave them that lovely name. No wonder they sold so well.

The singles came in 250, 350 and 500 cc sizes listed as the Tigers 70, 80 and 90 with the unspoken suggestion that the figures represented top speeds. Once the Speed Twin was in production in 1938, it came as no surprise that for 1939 the Tiger 90 single was replaced by a twin. It was another brilliant move to christen it the Tiger 100.

The T100, as it was listed, was much as the Speed Twin but had the stylish Tiger finish in silver sheen for the mudguards and tank panels with the remainder of the tank chrome plated. The wheel rims were also plated with lined silver centres and the headlamp plated as for the 5T.

In the engine there were high-compression pistons and polished ports while the silencers were a stroke of genius. Each was shaped like a megaphone yet with rounded ends plus tailpipes which were pleasing enough. The trick was that the removal of three screws allowed the end complete with internal pipe to come away leaving a plain, open megaphone!

There were detail changes as well with a larger carburettor and modified inlet manifold while the number plate surround and rear chain oiling, as on the 5T, went on the new model. The petrol tank capacity was increased but its knee grips were sunk into recesses to keep the width acceptable. The oil tank was enlarged to a full imperial gallon. A neat detail which was to remain a Triumph mainstay for many years was to mark the speedometer face with rpm scales for each of the four gears.

To supplement the megaphone silencers there was an option intended for racing in the form of an aluminium-bronze cylinder head, listed for an extra £5 in 1939. They are now rare and a special feature on any prewar Tiger 100.

There was to have been a Tiger 85 in 1940, and this used the engine construction later seen in the 1945 3T. The cycle parts were from the twin in the main, although the front brake and petrol tank came from the single-cylinder Tiger 80. The model was to

After 1959 the Bonneville had a separate headlamp shell. This is the final pre-unit model of 1962. It always offered tremendous performance from its lithe lines, and the duplex frame had improved the handling a little.

be announced the week that World War II broke out, but was cancelled although its presence was seen as a headline on a magazine cover. This caused some confusion when a few copies did go out with the description still in them; the rest had been revised.

The Tiger 85 was included in the model range announced in March 1945 but never went into production. The Tiger 100 did of course, and received the same changes as the Speed Twin with telescopic front forks, separate magneto and dynamo, 19 in. front wheel and rear-wheel-driven speedometer. The engine received the amendments to the rocker oiling system and breather, while the silencers became the standard tubular parts and no longer had their exciting megaphone shape.

An original 1949 TR5 Trophy after restoration, showing the square-finned, all-alloy engine with parallel ports and lovely exhaust pipe line. The frame was specially made to shorten the wheelbase. The result was a nice dual-purpose model which could take its owner to work during the week and then through a trial on the weekend. Desirable then and now.

The Tiger 100 mirrored the 5T up to 1950, with the sprung hub option in 1947 and the nacelle in 1949. The new gearbox was fitted for 1950 when the T100 joined the others in adopting the four-band tank styling, dual seat option and external rocker drain oil pipes. The early postwar Tigers were lovely machines with real performance and a muted snarl from the exhaust. It was not loud or offensive but purposeful, and it fit the name so well. For their day they were quick motorcycles and as fast on a journey as most others.

The T100 had a major engine change for 1951 when both head and barrel were changed to light alloy die castings with close-pitch fins. This had a major effect on the machine's appearance and was enhanced by fitting the dual seat as standard. The toolbox was moved to a new location above the upper chain stay, and the model received the same bayonet fitting filler cap as did the rest of the range.

The revised frame was used by the T100 for 1952 when it received the underslung pilot lamp and petrol tank with centre seam. For 1953 there was just the rectangular rear lamp, but 1954 brought major changes to both engine and frame. The engine was altered to the bigger timing-side main bearing plus the associated crankcase, while the frame was new with pivoted fork rear suspension. There was also a larger 8 in. front brake and a new finish in shell blue.

A second Tiger appeared that year in the form of the 649 cc Tiger 110 based on the Thunderbird engine, and this too used the new pivoted fork frame. The engine internals were uprated from the 6T ones to improve the performance, but the iron head and block remained. The T110 was fitted with the same 8 in. front brake and finished in the same colour and style as the smaller model.

The result was a really quick motorcycle that was lively to ride, for it retained the same frame. Even so, it hinged in the middle at speed, or if the rider changed up in a hurry, but it kept the Tiger snarl. Acceleration was extremely good even up steep hills while the machine retained its docile manners, thanks in part to the single carburettor.

The next year had both Tigers breathing through an Amal Monobloc, and they received the detail changes to the rear lamp and rear brake torque stay. For 1956 there was an alloy cylinder head for the T110 which dispensed with the external oil drains, while both models had a ventilated backplate for the front brake. Among the details, the underslung pilot lamp was replaced by a horn grill and the parcel grid was revised.

The new tank badges of grill form were adopted for 1957 when a return was made to the silver grey colour as standard, with the addition of an option in ivory and blue. A further option for the T100 only was a splayed-port cylinder head which went with a twin-carburettor set. Both models adopted the split fork ends.

A new full-width front hub was fitted for 1958, and although it retained the 8 in. brake this no longer had a vented backplate. The hub went on both models as did the Slick-shift gearbox and a steering lock, while the front mudguards adopted a deeper section and lost their front stay and the appropriate lug on the end of the forks. An optional splayed-port head appeared for the T110 and was joined by listed twin carburettors. Both Monobloc and Amal GP types were included for either capacity engine.

The outcome of higher performance was a new design of crankshaft for 1959, which was the last year for the Tiger 100. It was also the first year of a motorcycle legend, the T120 Bonneville, which was in essence a Tiger 110 fitted with the splayed-port head and twin carburettors. It also managed without the Slickshift but retained the nacelle and dynamo just as the other sports twins.

The T120 Bonneville also represented the first real step along the performance-at-all-costs road, and the more thoughtful doubted it was entirely a good thing for road use. Fine for racing of course, but the extra response and speed given by the added carburettor only remained as long as the engine was on top line. It was inevitably harder to set the twin units, and on the road the T110 was nearly as fast. It also tended to stay in tune longer, and a good T110 would always stay with a T120 needing attention.

Of course this had no effect at all on most buyers who went for the Bonneville in a big way, so Triumph made the right commercial decision even if for the wrong reasons. The T120 continued in this way right to the end to demonstrate the special thought needed to produce machines people buy.

There were some major changes for 1960. There was no T100, and the other models had a new duplex frame, and an alternator on the end of the crankshaft. They did keep their magnetos, but diverged in regard to appearance. The T110 was fitted with the bathtub over its rear end and so became a high-performance version of the 6T without any options, while the T120 abandoned the nacelle to take on a more sporting style.

The Bonneville was also built in two export styles for the United States. The first was the T120R, whose main changes were to raised bars and the appropriate longer cables. A competition magneto was fitted as well as a smaller three-gallon tank, but otherwise the machine was as the home market one.

The second machine was the Competition T120C that had a waist-level exhaust pipe and silencer on each side, and studded trail

By 1951 the TR5 has gained the diecast alloy head and barrel in common with the T100, but remained in its rigid frame and original format. It kept its light weight and stayed just as desirable. This one is on show in 1988.

The last year for the TR5 was 1958, by which time it had put on weight and length while the power curve had become sharper. This changed the way it worked, from the original soft and easy ride to a harder and harsher scrambles type of behaviour, which was not so pleasant.

tyres. For 1961 the two models were continued, the USA variants adding an undershield and wader magneto for the T120C.

At the end of 1961 the T110 was dropped as the 6T with alloy head took its place, so only the Bonneville continued for 1962. The home and two export versions remained, but at the end of the year all were replaced by machines with the new unit construction engine.

Prospects

As with the tourers, the T100 comes in two basic frame forms, but again both are desirable. The alloy engine is equally so but the older iron-engine models are rarer, which balances the issue.

The T100s all rate four stars, for sports models are always more collectible than tourers. The odd man out is the 1939 model, which has to be worth five stars since there are few left. If it has the bronze head then it rates five-plus stars. All are considered nice machines and good investments.

The early iron-head T110 is less favoured than later models because it still had the pivoted fork frame, so it gets three stars. The 1960-61 versions with bathtub rate the same, for they are nice motorcycles rather than ones people go for. The choicest versions are the alloy head models of 1956-59, which are rated four stars and worth putting your money on.

The classic T120 has to rate four stars minimum, for this is the one most people prefer. The 1959 model climbs to a five, as it differs from the rest and is a rare bird now. All T120s are excellent investments.

TR sports twins

These TR models, or sporting twins, were first introduced as dual-purpose machines in an era when one model had to take its owner to work during the week and through the trials on the weekends. It is a role now fulfilled by trail bikes, for trials have become too specialized.

Triumph based their model on the machines their works riders had used in the 1948 ISDT with success, and called it the TR5 Trophy. It used the Speed Twin engine

The larger 649 cc TR6 of 1958 used the same set of cycle parts as the TR5 but had a larger front brake. This example has the high bars and raised exhausts on each side for the American market, where it was successful as an off-road model.

The drive side of the TR6 of the 1958-59 period when it was still built as an off-road machine. It was thus suited to enduro events although its weight called for a good deal of strength to handle. This one has the siamesed exhaust pipes fitted for the home market.

with a square-finned, light alloy head and barrel taken from a wartime generator unit. Due to this ancestry the exhaust ports were parallel and led to a neat siamesed system mounted waist-high on the left of the machine.

The frame was specially made to reduce the wheelbase and to fit the engine snugly. The sprung hub was an option, but the short sporting mudguards were standard as was the 20 in. front wheel and 4 in. rear tyre. The headlamp was quickly detachable and the result was a handsome motorcycle. It alone went without the nacelle and was fitted with a saddle and pillion pad. It also proved to be a nice machine to ride on road or trail, for its light weight gave it good performance and the tyres did not inhibit it too much. Like all pre-unit Triumphs it would start easily and had that air of getting on with the job.

The TR5 was fitted with the revised gearbox for 1950 but retained its special wide ratios. It also kept its original tank style and finish, with chrome plating and silver panels matched by lined silver mudguards. For 1951 the engine top half was altered to use the diecast parts from the Tiger 100 with the close-pitch fins, and the exhaust pipes were modified to suit the splayed ports.

The model then continued with little change until 1954 when the big timing main went in with the crankcase to suit. It was revised more extensively the next year when it was given a pivoted fork frame and the four-bar tank styling, acquired the Monobloc carburettor in line with the range and had a dual seat as standard.

For 1956 the Trophy was joined by a second and larger version listed as the TR6 and fitted with the Tiger 110 649 cc engine with alloy head. This was to the same specification with the same cams and compression ratio, and reflected the changing role of the model. The TR5 had had a rise in ratio the previous year and thus both engines were now aimed far more to performance, and the machines were becoming street scramblers rather than trials irons. Somehow this did not seem to suit them at all and they lost something in style and performance over

For 1961 the TR6 became a road model and effectively a single-carburettor Bonneville with no relevance to the early off-road format. This 1962 version has a siamesed exhaust system and the model took over the role of the T110 by offering sports performance without the trauma of twin carbs.

the ground as opposed to simple performance. That year the two models were similar. Both had the 7 in. front brake and were
fitted with petrol tanks with a centre seam.

The tanks had the grill badges for 1957
plus forks with split clamp ends but different
front brakes. The TR5 kept to the 7 in. size
but changed to a full-width hub, whereas
the TR6 had the Tiger brake of 8 in. diameter with a ventilated backplate.

Both got the Slickshift in 1958, and the
TR6 changed to another front brake in line
with the Tigers', and fitted the full-width
hub with 8 in. brake without the vented
backplate. At the end of the year the TR5
was dropped but the larger model continued
with a stronger crankshaft.

It was given the new frame with duplex
downtubes for 1960, and also an alternator
although it continued to rely on the magneto
for ignition. Late in the year it was dropped
in its off-road form, but the model name was
revived early in 1961.

The 1961 Trophy was in a totally new
form for a TR model, for it was in essence a
single-carburettor T120 and thus replaced
the original form of the T110. As such it
became the performance model for the thinking man who wished to avoid the hassle of
carburettor balancing too often. For 1962 it
was listed as the TR6 S/S, lost its Slickshift
and was fitted with siamesed exhaust pipes
with the silencer low down on the right. In
this form it reached the end of its days as a
pre-unit model but was to continue on with
unit construction.

Prospects

The early TR5 model was one of the nicest
machines of all time, is rare and has a five-
star rating for the square-barrel model and
four stars for the 1951-54 editions. Both
have to be sure-fire investments. The 1955-
on type is less popular, as it moved away
from the original concept, and buyers for
that era often prefer the larger engine.

Thus the late-type TR5 rates three stars
while the TR6 of 1956-60 gets four, thanks
to its size and rarity. The road model of
1961-62 is a three-star, middle-of-the-road
machine because most riders prefer the
Bonneville. In fact the TR6 is much nicer for
general riding, only has the one carburettor

to keep up to the mark and is nearly as quick
in practical terms. Thus, if you are buying to
ride, the TR6 is a better bet even if it is less
likely to do more than maintain its price
level.

US Variants

Most models were available in a USA form
that usually comprised high bars and suita-
bly long control cables, maybe a smaller
petrol tank but seldom any change in colour
or basic specification. As time went by the
changes grew and by 1960 there were distinct
models for the USA only, some being produced in East and West Coast forms to suit
market needs separated by some 3,000 miles.

In 1960, this introduced four models, all of
649 cc, and based on the home market T120
and TR6 machines. The twin-carburettor
models were the TR7/A and TR7/B while
those with one carburettor were the TR6/A
and TR6/B. The /A models were listed as
Road Sports machines and were essentially
as the stock models with low-level exhaust
systems, ribbed front tyre and the usual
sports mudguards. Changes amounted to
high bars and the rev-counter fitted as
standard.

The /B models were listed as Scramblers
and set up for off-road or trail use, fitted with
trials tyres, a waist-level exhaust system on
each side and the high bars. Only a speedometer was supplied while the finish was
blue and grey for the TR7, red and ivory for
the TR6.

All four models changed codes for 1961, the
TR7/A becoming the T120/R, the TR7/B the
T120/C, the TR6/A the TR6/R and the TR6/B
the TR6/C. In essence they were unaltered
but a wide-ratio gearset went into the off-
road models and the finishes were new. The
T120 machines were in blue and silver while
the TR6 became ruby red and silver.

The US lists included both the 6T and T110
in standard and economy versions that year,
the latter in the 1960 finish and no doubt left
over from the previous season. For 1962 the
variants received the general changes but
otherwise stayed as they were.

Prospects

Four stars for all as these models are rare.
They were built for a short time only and for
one market.

Chapter 2

Small unit twins

★★★	3TA Twenty-one 1957-58
★★	3TA Twenty-one 1959-63
★	3TA Twenty-one 1964-66
★★★	5TA Speed Twin 1959-63
★★	5TA Speed Twin 1964-66
★★★	T90 Tiger 90 1963
★★	T90 Tiger 90 1964-69
★★★	T100A Tiger 100 1960-61
★★★★	T100SS Tiger 100 1962-63
★★★	T100SS Tiger 100 1964-65
★★★	T100 Tiger 100 1966
★★★	T100S Tiger 100 1967-70
★★★★	T100T Daytona 1967-70
★★★★	T100R Daytona 1966-69
★★★★	T100R Daytona 1971-74
★★★	T100C Trophy 1966-69
★★★	T100C Trophy 1971-72
★★★	TR5T Trophy Trail 1973-74

Triumph moved over to unit construction in 1957 and with it adopted a new enclosed form of styling and a return to the 350 cc class. Both were to go in time, in response to buyer's demands, but for a period the model's elegant and unique lines enhanced the range.

The first model was called the Twenty-One or T21, but within a year or so was listed as the 3TA. It was a new design but retained much of the past in its layout and looks, so the camshafts were still in the same places, the gear drive to them was laid out as before and the valve gear followed familiar Triumph lines.

Edward Turner on a 5TA leads a number of industry and press figures off for a ride on the unit models and at least one Cub. Period riding gear for all, and machines that had a new style but the old Triumph line.

The engine looked all-alloy but, while the head was in this material, the block was cast iron painted silver. The usual Triumph pushrod covers went fore and aft of it, and two separate rocker boxes sat on top of the head. A manifold carried a single Amal Monobloc carburettor, and on the exhaust side there were screwed-in adapters in the ports to which the pipes were fixed with finned clamps.

In the bottom half of the 3TA went a one-piece crankshaft, with bolted-on flywheel, and connecting rods with split big ends. A ball race served as the drive main but there was a plain bush on the timing side. The oil pump continued to be driven by the inlet camshaft nut and the breather by the left end of the inlet camshaft itself.

Only in the electrical department was there some novelty, although the alternator on the left end of the crankshaft was the normal Lucas component. Different was the housing for the points and distributor, which was located behind the right cylinder where it was skew-gear-driven from the

The smaller 349 cc 3TA was introduced during 1957. This 1961 example has an added screen. The model also brought in the bathtub and retained the nacelle to present a smooth face to the world. The scene is typical of the time.

inlet camshaft. The high-tension leads thus rose in a fine sweep from the cap to curl forward over the engine, where they split off to the cylinders and the coil.

The 5TA Speed Twin was introduced in 1959 to replace the old 5T and was hard to distinguish from the smaller 3TA. It kept the Amaranth Red finish, but the badges differed and there were

other alterations inside the engine. It is less easy to alter a 3TA to a 5TA than appears at first sight. Another engine is really the best way.

By 1964 the 3TA was dropping its touring image by wearing a skirt in place of the bathtub. As this had been a sports fitment, it meant the model rather fell between two buying stools. But the movement of the contact points to the timing cover had to be an improvement over the old distributor.

Thus there was little that was radical in the internals or the top half of the new engine, and the crankcase retained its vertical joint line. This was still on the centre line of the engine, but then staggered to the left

so that the whole of the gearbox was contained in the right crankcase casting. The left casting was extended back to form the inner primary chaincase, with a further outer cover to enclose the duplex chain drive, clutch and alternator.

The primary drive was thus on fixed centres and the chain had no means of adjustment or tensioning. The four-speed gearbox was laid out with the shafts one behind the other, but was otherwise of conventional English form. The whole assembly including the selectors and their camplate could be built up on the gearbox inner cover, which went on the right of the main casting. It could then be offered up as one to the case, whether the left side was in position or not, as long as the sleeve gear was in place. The output sprocket and primary drive would then have to be added later.

There was an outer cover for the gearbox on the right and this was shaped to blend in with the timing cover which was of triangular form. Once all the castings were together

The tourers' last year was 1966 and both the 3TA shown here, and the 5TA, had lost their skirts. They were thus little different from the Tiger models, but did retain the nacelle and a charm of their own on the road.

the result was a smooth, sleek engine unit that still retained its unmistakable Triumph line.

The cycle side was rather basic, with a loop frame with duplex rails beneath the engine unit and bolted-on subframe. The headstock was poorly supported, and pivoted fork rear suspension was provided. On these bare bones were hung the clothes that gave the machine its line and style, even if beneath them there was inadequacy in the provisions for handling.

At the front there were the usual Triumph forks complete with nacelle carrying the headlamp, switches and instruments. The front wheel had a nice full-width hub and a simple, single-leading shoe brake, but at the rear went the usual hub. Far less common for the times was the use of 17 in. rims for both wheels and these carried 3.25 in. section tyres front and rear.

Style came from the deeply valanced front mudguard with just a rear stay and, of course, from the famous bathtub rear enclosure. This ran back from the carburettor to the rear number plate and down from the seat to wheel spindle level. It did however leave the wheel in view, and this cutout removed any suggestion of slab-sidedness and kept the light, nearly dainty look common to the marque. It also promoted the nickname, for the enclosure did indeed look like an old-fashioned hip bath inverted for the machine.

The seat hinged down on top of the bathtub and was secured by a catch while beneath it went a moulded rubber pad designed to carry the tools in slots and recesses. A plain inner mudguard kept the worst of the weather away from the seat and moulding. Under the seat were also the oil tank, battery, air filter and electrical components.

The launch model was finished in silver-grey, but for production the major parts such as tank, front mudguard, enclosure and forks were in shell blue and the other painted parts in black.

From the 3TA sprang a whole line of machines of both 350 and 500 cc. At first the accent was on tourers, but before long these were joined by a sports model, and during the 1960s the pendulum swung away from

The first unit Tiger was the T100A with bathtub, here seen in its 1961 finish. It lacked the style of the original, for it was hard to tell apart from the Speed Twin and had few real sporting pretensions.

the 3TA concept to super sports machines. One result was the Daytona, a fast 500, and another the Adventurer, an off-road model that came along later.

Touring models

There were two tourers, one the original 349 cc 3TA and the other the 490 cc 5TA. Except for colour, they tended to be like two peas in a pod and a good many 3TA owners have changed enough parts to create a 5TA. Beware of these, as the full list of engine changes is significantly long and not all may have been included.

The 5TA first appeared for 1959 and was finished in the traditional Amaranth Red for all painted parts. The engine items that differed from those in the 3TA were the block, pistons, cylinder head, valves, valve springs, connecting rods, pushrods and small end bushes. Other items changed were the gearbox sprocket, motifs on the rear enclosure, carburettor size and settings, distributor spring set, rear suspension units and the rear tyre which was increased in section to 3.50 in. A few of those parts are hard to check and could have a significant effect on the final result.

Otherwise, the two machines were the same and performed smoothly enough in either size. The handling was not a strong

The T100SS had more sporting lines with its abbreviated skirt and separate headlamp shell finished with chrome plating. This 1962 model retained the distributor behind the block and so had its ignition problems, which were solved the next year when the points moved.

point but buyers tended to be more interested in the enclosure and touring aspects, so this was not a problem. If the machine was not pressed too hard it performed well

Triumph models on display in France in 1964 with a Tiger model to the front. By then the styling move was away from enclosure to the cafe racer form, which ran through the 1960s although Triumph still used the bathtub on the tourers.

enough and its detail fittings and fixtures suited the intended customer. It was 1960 before either the 3TA or 5TA had any changes, and the first of these was to the bathtub whose joint flanges were reversed so they pointed outward and the bolts became visible—easier to deal with but not so tidy and neat. The other change was the addition of a primary chain tensioner, but for the 5TA only.

The 3TA had to wait until 1961 before it too gained the tensioner, and that year both models lost the tool pad from beneath the dual seat. In its place there was a tool bag and a metal carrier for it to fit into, while the petrol tank had optional styling strips. If fitted, these ran fore and aft of the tank badges and were intended for other models with a two-tone tank finish where they went over the paint join.

Both models were fitted with siamesed exhaust pipes for 1962, with these feeding into a low-mounted silencer on the right. Both changed back to the original system the next year. They received more noticeable changes for 1964 when the distributor was deleted and the points moved into the timing chest, where their cam was driven from the exhaust camshaft. At the same time the bathtub was replaced by a skirt that only partly enclosed the rear wheel, and the front forks were revised.

The front mudguard was altered for 1965 to lose its valance and take on a more sporting line, while the frame was stiffened by a brace bolted between the headstock and the seat nose. For 1966 this was welded into place and the skirt deleted, so the machines were given a side panel to enclose the left side and match the oil tank.

The 3TA and 5TA also went to 18 in. wheels, a twelve-volt electric system and a new tank badge of eyebrow style, but at the end of the season both were dropped. Sports models were in and tourers were out.

Prospects

Low ratings for the tourers simply reflect people's preference for models that are either bigger, more sporting or both. The 350 cc rates lower than the 500 except for the opening years when only the smaller one was available, and both rate lower for the years after they had lost their bathtubs.

So three stars are awarded to the 3TA from 1957-59, but only two for 1960-63 and one for 1964-66. The 5TA rates three for 1959-63 and two from then on, but the later models are no less pleasant to own and ride. Remember that replacement bathtubs are hard to find, so do not be too tempted by an early model that lacks one.

This could all change though, since complete bathtub models in original condition are few and hard to restore if parts are lacking. This may make them desirable and collectable in the future, so they could be a reasonable long shot, and meanwhile nice to ride—but don't let the tub deteriorate.

If you simply want one to ride, then buy one. These factors override all others in evaluating motorcycling as a pastime.

Sports models

The sports models range from the T100A with its tourer appearance via the skirted models to the full-blown super sports Daytona. Right at the end of their production came a single off-road model which used the smaller twin unit.

The T100A made its debut in 1960 and carried the Tiger 100 name from the past, although it lacked the earlier style. In truth,

The 1965 Tiger 90, which offered some performance from its modest capacity but in a frame that was a trifle uneasy with the power. It was none too popular. Riders looking for power chose the larger models and those wishing to tour preferred the softer and easier Speed Twin.

The 1965 T100SS placed high demands on the frame which was still in trouble despite the addition of a top bracing strut. It was a keen middleweight contender and a popular machine despite the indifferent handling. The ignition was no longer a problem although the electrics were still six-volt.

it was hard to distinguish it from the tourers other than by its two-tone tank finish and bathtub badges.

Nearly all the differences were on the inside, for the engine had high-compression pistons, hotter camshafts and the painful energy transfer ignition. This last meant a

Changes for export were really quite minimal in many cases, as this 1966 Western T100C for the USA shows. It had a raised siamesed exhaust system reminiscent of the early TR5, small headlamp and suitable wheels and tyres. Most parts were common to the standard T100.

special alternator and coil plus revised distributor with different cam. These electrics were controlled with a cutout button in the nacelle, so the usual combined light and ignition switch with key was replaced by a simple switch for the lights.

This was the only obvious external difference, although the silencers had mutes fitted in their ends as standard. The model had the same carburettor as the 5TA for that first year, an Amal Monobloc type 375/35, but was given an extra pair of plates in the clutch to deal with the power.

The carburettor was changed to a larger-type Amal 376/273 for 1961. The only other alterations were to delete the moulded rubber tool pad and change the lower tank colour from ivory to silver; this was used for the front mudguard and rear enclosure as well. During the year, at engine number H22430, the energy transfer ignition system was dropped and the T100A fitted with the parts and switches as used by the 5TA. At the end of the season the T100A was dropped and thus had a brief run by Triumph twin standards. It really did not warrant the Tiger label at all, as it completely failed to fit the image it evoked, being too stodgy.

For 1962 it was replaced by the T100SS model which was much better and had nice sporting lines. This used the T100A engine with a change of exhaust camshaft and the normal coil ignition system, plus most of the same cycle parts. The changes were to the exhaust pipes which were joined to run to a low-mounted silencer on the right, the forks which carried a separate chrome-plated headlamp shell and were fitted with gaiters, and the rear enclosure. This last was reduced to a skirt which left the whole of the rear wheel exposed. Due to this a normal rear mudguard was fitted. This gave the T100SS style in the old manner and excited riders just by standing in front of one.

The T100SS had the points moved into the timing case for 1963 when it was joined by the smaller-capacity Tiger 90. This repeated the sports form and thus used the same cycle parts. Into them went the 349 cc engine fitted with high-compression pistons

and the T100SS camshafts. The carburettor was larger than that of the tourers and the gearing was to suit the power output and speed. Otherwise only the finish and badges distinguished the two sports twins.

Both had the revised front forks for 1964 and a change in styling. The skirts were discontinued and a left side panel was used to match the oil tank and enclose the electrics in that area. The siamesed pipes were also deleted, and the more usual twin low-level systems were fitted in their place.

The frame was fitted with the bolted-in bracing strut between headstock and seat nose for 1965. This was the last year for the T100SS. The T90 continued with the strut welded in place for 1966 and that year was joined by four versions of the Tiger 100— the T100, T100R and two T100Cs.

All had the same basic engine and gearbox which went in the same frame and forks as the T90. The T100 was the base home model and, as with all that year, had twelve-volt electrics and the eyebrow-style tank badge. A minor change was that the rear chain oil

The home-market models had many common parts as seen on this 1967 Tiger 90. This continued in the range, although riders preferred the larger T100, and by then had an improved frame and forks. Nice to ride within its limitations.

The more popular 1967 Tiger 100 which had the new frame and better forks along with a change of tank badge in 1966. It shared chassis parts with the smaller model, and oil tank badges and colour were often the only way to tell the two machines apart.

feed was taken from the oil tank return line instead of the primary chaincase, so the correct tank has an adjuster in its filler neck.

The other three versions of the Tiger 100 were for the United States. Nearest in looks to the home model was the T100R. This had trail tyres with a 19 in. front rim in place of the usual 18 in., and a 4.00 in. section rear tyre. It was fitted with raised bars and ball-ended clutch and brake levers, plus a small petrol tank and a rev counter.

The other two were Eastern and Western editions of the T100C which had alternator electrics, small headlamp and siamesed exhaust pipes connected to a waist-level silencer on the left. They also had the small tank, an undershield and folding footpegs, and the Western model had light alloy mudguards, or fenders as they were known in the United States.

The Eastern model was fitted as standard with the wide-ratio gears which, like the close gear set, were an option for the sports twins. It also had different front fork damping and a black seat top in place of the standard grey.

The T90 had a new seat with ribs and a slight tail for 1967, as did the larger home model which became the T100S. All models finally received a much needed revised frame with a full-size top tube and the bracing tube beneath it rather than the other way round. The existing models were joined by others and the most exciting was the T100T Daytona. This had twin carburettors to uprate its performance to a high level plus a rev counter to enable the rider to keep an eye on things.

The T100T was in total contrast to the first unit construction twin of a decade before, which had aimed to keep the works decorously out of sight and the performance in the touring image. The high engine speeds soon began to take their toll in fractured hardware. But it was what the market wanted, although in decline at the time.

The same engine and both carburettors went into the T100R which also received a ribbed front tyre and the new seat as did the T100C. There was only one version of this listed, and it came with the standard gear ratios although both wide and close sets remained available. Its exhaust system was altered to separate pipes and silencers but these remained on the left at waist level, one above the other.

All models changed over to Amal Concentric carburettors for 1968 and had the primary chaincase altered to provide an access cover over the alternator rotor. This allowed the ignition timing to be checked with a strobe light which was a useful facility. Also on the electrical side was the use of a finned heat sink mounting for the zener diode in place of the earlier flat plate. Both twin-carburettor models had their front brakes increased to 8 in. but they still remained of the single-leading-shoe type. All models lost the covers from their rear suspension units.

The four T100 models plus the T90 continued for 1969 and all were fitted with twin-leading-shoe front brakes. The T100T and T100R kept their 8 in. diameter front brakes while the other models retained the 7 in. A new picture frame badge went on the tank, and a pressure switch in the timing cover for the oil was added, which included a warning light in the headlamp shell.

The exhaust pipes gained a balance pipe between them close to the exhaust port, and for the T100C there was a connector with cross pipe which went between the exhausts and the silencers. These were also fitted with a wire grill heat shield.

The T90 was dropped at the end of 1969, for performance buyers always went for the larger capacity machine, and the C and R versions of the T100 for the United States were no longer listed for 1970. There were few changes that year other than to the engine breather, which meant a tube was run from the top rear inner face of the primary chaincase while a grab rail was added to the rear mudguard stay to run up behind the dual seat.

The type numbers were reversed for 1971, the year the group made a major marketing launch, with no S or T model but the reappearance of the C and R models in their place. They were much as before, although the R now carried turn indicators and both had side reflectors fore and aft as required by USA legislation. For the home market the

R model was fitted with megaphone-style silencers.

The firm was by now in dire straits and work was concentrated on the larger models which were in major trouble. Thus the two Tiger 100 models were left alone for 1972, and for 1973 only the T100R was listed with just a change to the tank style and finish.

The T100C was replaced by the Trophy Trail TR5T, or Adventurer, for 1973 and this was aimed far more at the off-road enthusiast, unlike the earlier machine which was more of a street scrambler. The TR5T revived old memories of the original Trophy model of 1949 by using a somewhat similar tank finish plus more sporting wheels and mudguards.

The engine was the usual single-carburettor 490 cc twin but did have points-triggered capacitor ignition powered by the alternator. The transmission was as always but with wider gearbox ratios, and most of the chassis side was new to a Triumph 500.

Much of the cycle side came from the common selection of BSA and Triumph

The off-road T100C was firmly based on the road model for all years, and by 1970 had this nice line in pipes and silencers on the left. It also had the bellcrank twin-leading-shoe front brake, which could be excessive off-road, and bars, tank and wheels to suit.

The 1971 twin-carburettor T100R Daytona model, which offered considerable performance from its 490 cc engine. It kept its earlier frame and thus avoided the seat height problem of the 650s of that year, so remained a firm favourite with buyers.

The 1973 TR5T sold as the Adventurer or the Trophy Trail but lacked the charm and style of the old TR5. Off-road performance depends on some subtle engine factors, so the use of a detuned hot road unit may not be the answer. The exhaust pipes were an aesthetic disaster.

parts, with the frame derived from the BSA works scrambler. It was the frame also used by the BSA singles from 1971 on, with single top and down tubes joined by duplex ones, and in them went the engine oil. The pivoted rear fork supported the wheel at a fixed point and was itself moved to and fro for chain adjustment with a locating device at the pivot point. The front forks were of the slimline style without gaiters, had the wheel spindle caps held on four studs each and supported the small headlamp shell on bent wires.

The shell carried a turn indicator on each side while above it went both speedometer and rev counter. Behind it went a light alloy fuel tank with yellow side panels and aft of that, the dual seat. The machine rode on a 21 in. front wheel and 18 in. rear, while both tyres were suited to trail use and the mudguards were held well clear of them. Both wheels had conical hubs with single-leading-shoe brakes, with an 8 in. brake at the front and 7 in. at the rear.

The exhaust system lacked the style of the old TR5 or even the later T100C models; the two pipes simply ran down to join in front of the frame at a low level. A single pipe then ran under the engine to a box silencer, and this area was protected by an undershield. The whole assembly looked wrong for an off-road model and did nothing to excite a prospective buyer.

During 1973 the future of the Triumph works at Meriden became much involved with politics and the Norton-Villiers group. As a result the NVT group was formed, which included Triumph, and the discussions included a cash subsidy from the Department of Trade. The outcome in September was the announcement that Meriden would be closed and production transferred to the BSA works at Small Heath.

The reaction of the work force was disgust at their treatment and they responded by locking the factory gates and staging their famous sit-in. This ran on into 1975 before it was resolved.

Thus, although there are parts lists for the T100R and TR5T for 1974, there were effectively few machines built in that period, and those were as in 1973. Some may have appeared in the shops in 1975 but were old stock; after the sit-in the factory built only the larger twins.

Prospects

Mainly three stars for the sports models group, as the smaller models never do as well as the larger even though they are often nicer to ride and easier to handle. So, if you enjoy your riding, any unit T100 will make a nice mount, even if a little harsher than the older pre-unit one.

The Tiger 90 drops to two stars for 1964 on, when it lost its skirt and became just a small Tiger. But it will still make a nice model. Even so, most of us prefer more capacity and the easier engine note when cruising. In contrast, the T100SS for 1961-63 rates a four because of its sheer style which makes it that little bit better than the others. The T100A ought to do better as a short-run model but seems to fall between too many stools, for the enclosure will appeal to tourers and for them the 5T or 6T

could be preferred. For sheer lazy performance in the bathtub the later T110 would be the model rather than the T100A.

Later exceptions to the three stars have to be the twin-carburettor Daytona models— the T100T and T100R. They represent the top of the range in the 500 cc class, and in a field of performance models would be the ones to seek. Whether the R or C models are more desirable than the S or T depends on which side of the Atlantic you live on, plus what you can find. All should be good investments, since power always attracts.

The TR5T ought to rate more than three, if only for its rarity, but somehow it fails to click. Once more it is a case of a nice machine if you want one, but unlikely to do more than keep up with the market.

US Variants

The TR series in 490 cc, unit-construction form first appeared in 1961 as the TR5A/R and TR5A/C models. They repeated the road and trail formats of the larger twins using the sports version of the engine as fitted to the T100A and mirrored the other TR models in their style and equipment.

The road machine was the TR5A/R, which was in a form the T100 was to take later without the bathtub or skirt rear enclosure. It had energy-transfer ignition, sports mudguards, road tyres, low-level exhausts and a rev-counter as standard.

The Enduro Trophy TR5A/C was much the same but with off-road tyres, lower gearing, wide-ratio gearset and small headlamp. Its frame was braced with a strut (not to appear at home until 1965), there was an undershield, a smaller petrol tank and siamesed exhaust pipes leading to a short, low-level silencer on the right. There was only a speedometer and no centre stand.

Both models had a list of options including a race kit to convert to class C or dirt track specification. They were finished in Kingfisher blue and silver. The doubtful energy-transfer system was replaced by coil ignition on the road model during 1961 and this was the only one of the pair to continue for 1962, the off-road model becoming the T100SC, both finished in burgundy and silver.

For 1963 the TR5A/R became the T100SR

and both it and the T100SC had the general range changes of timing cover points and three-spring clutch. Both models adopted the rear skirt, as used by the home-market T100SS. The exhaust remained as before along with the high bars, the T100SC kept the energy-transfer ignition system and the finish that year was in Regal purple and silver.

Both models lost their skirts for 1964 when the exhaust on the off-road model was changed to a waist-level silencer on the left, still connected to siamesed pipes. The finish for both became sapphire red and silver but polished aluminum mudguards went on the T100SC.

They continued as they were for 1965, the finish that year being gold and white, after which the models were replaced by the general export T100R and T100C machines that continued to 1972. The off-road model then became the TR5T and both ran on to the end of production of the small unit twins.

Prospects

Three stars rising for rarity. A few of these machines have made it back to their homeland, but they were never too common. Could appreciate more except that owners seem to prefer the larger-capacity twins and pre-unit styling. The small unit twins tend to be bland and less popular while remaining pleasant machines to ride.

Chapter 3

Large unit twins

★★★	6T Thunderbird 1963-65
★★	6T Thunderbird 1966
★★★	TR6 Trophy 1963-70
★★★	TR6R Trophy 1966-70
★★★	TR6R Tiger 1971-73
★★★	TR6C Trophy 1966-67
★★★	TR6C Trophy 1971-73
★★★	TR6RV Tiger 1972-73
★★★	TR6CV Trophy 1972-73
★★★	TR7RV Tiger 1973-75
★★★★	T120 Bonneville 1963-70
★★★★★	T120 Thruxton 1965
★★★★	T120R Bonneville 1963-70
★★★★	T120R Bonneville 1971-73
★★★★	T120C Bonneville 1963-65
★★★★	T120TT Bonneville 1964-67
★★★★	T120V Bonneville 1972-75
★★★★	T120RV Bonneville 1972-75
★★★★	T140V Bonneville 1973-75
★★★★	T140RV Bonneville 1973-75

Once all the smaller twins had changed over to unit construction it was only a matter of time before the larger ones followed suit. The expected announcement came late in 1962, when the next season's models were shown, and the twin moved on to what was to be its final form.

There were three models in the line-up, aimed at the touring, sports and super sports markets, and they retained the names of the past as Thunderbird, Trophy and Bonneville or 6T, TR6 and T120 respectively. All used the same basic engine unit, frame, forks, wheels and many detail parts. Differences were relatively minor ones in specification and styling.

With the introduction of unit construction for the 649 cc engine in 1963, the Thunderbird was the only one of the large twins to retain any rear enclosure. This was amended to the skirt type, and the model was also the only big twin to keep the nacelle.

Touring and sports models

The engine unit used much of the rotating mechanicals from the pre-unit machines, so there was not a great deal of change for them. The crankshaft continued as a one-piece forging with the flywheel bolted to it and still turned in a pair of races. The timing gear was still a train of gears driving two camshafts fore and aft, while these still drove the breather valve from the end of the inlet and a rev counter from the exhaust, except on the 6T.

New was the drive to the points cam from the right end of the exhaust camshaft, for the contacts were now in the timing cover just as on the small twins that year. An expected move, but the oil pump stayed where it was and the valve gear was just as before including the pushrod tubes.

The rods and pistons continued as they were as did most of the top half. The block was still held down by eight studs, the head was in light alloy and the two rocker boxes fitted to it with the access caps to the valve adjusters as before. The one change was an additional bolt to hold the head to the block, and this went between the cylinder bores to give the nine-stud head.

Specification differences between the models were lower-ratio pistons for the 6T which also had different camshafts and connecting rods. For the T120 there was still a twin-carburettor cylinder head but otherwise this engine was as the TR6, although the latter kept its siamesed exhaust pipes and low-mounted silencer on the right.

The major change was to the crankcase which was extended back to include the gearbox on the same lines as the smaller twins. Thus the crankcase continued to divide along the engine centre line but the joint was moved to the left, so the whole of the gearbox lay in the right case half. The left case now included the primary chaincase inner, with a large access hole to the gearbox sprocket, and the mountings for a chain tensioner.

Just as on the smaller twins, the timing chest was enclosed by a cover carrying the contact breakers, and the gearbox had inner and outer covers with the latter blended into the timing chest.

The primary drive became a duplex chain but otherwise was as before with a shock absorber built into the clutch centre. There were four speeds in the gearbox, and the construction did not follow the smaller

Despite the problem of keeping the carburettors in sync, the Bonneville stayed the preferred machine of the Triumph unit 650 twins; this is its 1963 form. It shared many parts from engine and frame with the other two models.

models but kept the layshaft beneath the mainshaft. The selectors and change mechanism continued as they were, so the box still had to be built up in the case rather than on the bench into the inner cover.

With the points in the timing cover there was no more magneto ignition, and the alternator had been in place since 1960 anyway. The electrics were still on six volts and

The pleasant TR6 in its first 1963 year with unit construction and a siamesed exhaust system. The single carburettor gave it more than adequate performance without the need to balance units as on the T120.

650 c.c. TRIUMPH THUNDERBIRD (6T)

The final 1966 version of the Thunderbird kept the nacelle but dispensed with the skirt, so was more like the TR6 than before. It offered good touring performance, but at a time when few buyers bought a 650 for anything other than performance.

There was a new frame for the new engine, with a single loop except for the twin tubes beneath the engine unit. The rear subframe bolted into place and the rear fork fitted between the ears of a major frame lug. This was still none too well supported to deal with the loads it had to carry, but at least the rear fork could be more easily removed for the fitting of new bushes.

Most other Triumph frames with pivoted fork rear suspension have the fork bushes straddling the frame and working on a pin pressed into the frame lug. Re-bushing requires the pin to be pressed out and it can be a major job without a good workshop. This has been mentioned before, but is a point worth repeating and one to beware of when buying and to watch for during ownership.

In other respects the frame was conventional, as were the forks. As mentioned, the 6T continued with the nacelle while the TR6 and T120 had a separate headlamp carrying the ammeter. For them the speedometer and rev counter sat side-by-side on a single the 6T carried its switches in the nacelle, while the others had theirs mounted in the left side panel just below the seat nose.

For 1966 there was a new tank badge and twelve-volt electrics. This TR6 offered a fine balance of performance with good petrol consumption and easy maintenance. The fork gaiters helped to stop the forks from being damaged and the parcel grid remained a popular feature.

bracket when the option was ordered, but otherwise there was just the speedometer on its bracket.

The sporting models had gaiters on their forks to suit their style and this was also reflected in the wheels and mudguards. All models had an 8 in. front brake in a full-width hub and a 7 in. rear in an offset one with an 18 in. rear wheel. The TR6 alone had a 4.00 in. section rear tyre and also a 19 in. front rim, the other two having 18 in. rims to match the rear.

The sports models had mudguards to suit but the Thunderbird kept to the deeply valanced form of the past. At the rear it lost its bathtub and put on a skirt in the style used by the smaller twins and thus gained a rear mudguard but kept its touring lines compared with the other models.

The petrol tank, complete with parcel grid, was common to all models as was the oil tank, battery carrier, seat and the standard bars, but the TR6 had ball-ended clutch and brake levers. There were American bars listed for all three models along with extended control cables.

This was the major alteration for the T120R built for the United States, along with the TR6 wheel sizes and the air filters seldom seen on a home market model. There was also a T120C which had a waist-level exhaust pipe and silencer on each side and, when built for the West Coast, usually had open pipes and no headlamp or number plates.

All the models managed to retain the Triumph look, although to some riders they had lost a trace of the earlier style and charm. They looked just a little bit heavier and so lacked the dainty air of the original. In addition, the ever-rising engine speeds, allied to the 649 cc capacity, began to result in an increasing number of brackets with fractures or splits.

There were revised front forks for all models in 1964 when the 6T changed to a twelve-volt electric system and gained a second battery and a zener diode mounted on a flat plate under the front of the petrol tank. The TR6 adopted the twin exhaust pipes and silencers of the T120, which was fitted with a balance pipe between its inlet tracts. The

For the Eastern USA version of the 1966 TR6C there were lights and waist-level exhaust pipes on each side with silencers. The model kept the small off-road headlamp and had raised bars and wheels and tyres to suit its use.

The 1966 Bonneville T120TT was an off-road racing machine and was fitted with a tuned engine with a high compression ratio. There were also well-tucked-in open pipes, while all the road equipment was removed to leave a stark and purposeful machine.

American T120 models continued along with a TT version, with an 11:1 compression ratio and energy transfer ignition.

The 6T was altered little for 1965, although a timing slot was machined into the flywheel and a tapped boss appeared in the crankcase behind the block to go with it. By inserting a pin, the engine could be locked at top dead centre.

A further version of the T120 was offered as the Thruxton Bonneville, built for production racing. Thus, it came with performance parts in the engine, rearsets and fairing, but was only available for a few months. All the extras were in fact listed, even if some were hard to find, and production racers preferred to add what they wanted rather than buy a package that might not be quite right.

There were more changes for 1966 when the eyebrow tank badge came in. All models now had the speedometer driven from the rear wheel, and the oil feed for the rear chain taken from the oil tank and metered with a screw under the filler cap. The TR6 and T120 joined the 6T in having twelve-volt electrics while the Thunderbird lost its skirt and gained a side panel. This went on the left to match the oil tank but was plain, without switches, as these remained in the nacelle.

The American Bonnevilles were listed as the T120R, very much as the home market model, and the T120TT with high ratio,

This is the standard Bonneville for 1967 when it still had Amal Monobloc carburettors and the single-leading-shoe front brake. By this time the handling was much improved, so slowing down was the only problem area aside from the vibration inherent in the vertical twin engine.

open pipes and no lights. The Trophy was also listed in various forms for the United States, with the TR6R much as the T120R. The TR6C was built in eastern form with trail tyres, small headlight and a waist-level exhaust pipe and silencer on each side. The western form was more off-road with no lights and both open pipes on the left at waist height. There was also a 6T for the United States, with high bars, sport mudguards and new rear light, but it kept the nacelle.

The Thunderbird was dropped from the line-up at the end of the season and with it went the Triumph nacelle that had given the range a special style for so long. Left were the sports models with a new ribbed seat, a steering lock in the top fork yoke and the lighting switch in the headlamp shell. For the TR6C, now in one version only, there was a silencer on the end of each exhaust pipe with both still at waist level on the left.

The models were reduced to the T120 and TR6 for 1968, plus the R type United States version which had minimal alterations. New for all models were Amal Concentric carbu-

TRIUMPH TROPHY 650

The massive model launch for 1971 introduced many new features for the 650s and included the infamous frame which carried the oil and increased the seat height far too much. This TR6C has a stylish exhaust system and is otherwise much as the T120.

rettors, the finned heat sink for the zener diode, an access cover in the primary chaincase outer and a twin-leading shoe front brake. This last had a straight operating

Braking for the 650 twins was improved with twin-leading-shoes at the front from 1968. This 1970 TR6 has the modified design with bell-crank lever. It is not as rigid as the original but makes for a neater cable. Carburettor had become an Amal Concentric and the rear units lost their covers to give the seals a harder time.

lever for that year, with the cable sweeping in from the rear.

The brake was revised for 1969 to a bell-crank lever to actuate the front cam and the cable led down the fork leg. At the same time the tank badge changed to the picture-frame type, all models lost their rear suspension unit covers, an oil-pressure switch was added and a balance pipe went between the exhausts, close up to the ports. For the T120 there were twin, windtone horns to aid the rider to clear his path.

The engine breather was altered for 1970, so a pipe appeared on the inner side of the primary chaincase at the top rear to carry the air away. Otherwise the models continued with little alteration, as the factory was heavily involved with its new range for 1971.

This was launched in great style and introduced the infamously high frame, new forks and conical hubs. There were three models for 1971, all much the same, listed as the TR6R, T120R and TR6C, with the first two being road models and differing only in having one or two carburettors.

The 1971 Bonneville shared much with the TR6 models, including the seat height, slimline forks and conical hubs. These housed new brakes and the front twin-leading-shoes were not effective because their levers were too short. The bent wire headlamp mounting was not popular and the indicators worked only when they wished.

First year for the larger 744 cc T140 Bonneville was 1972, when it used the same cycle parts as the T120 including the drum front brake. Early machines had a 725 cc capacity and later ones a five-speed gearbox option.

The engine was essentially the same but had modifications forced on it to suit its assembly to the new frame. This was totally different from the old one with large diameter top and seat tubes, which also acted as the oil tank, duplex downtubes which ran under the engine and a welded-on subframe. The rear fork was also new, along with most of the detail fittings.

The new front forks were in the slimline style with exposed stanchions and seal covers in place of the gaiters of the past. The fork internals were also new, while the wheel spindle caps were each held on by four studs. The headlamp was supported from the forks by two pieces of bent wire held in rubber bushes.

Both hubs were of the conical form with 8 in. front and 7 in. rear brakes and the front one also had twin-leading shoes. These were moved by two short levers pulled together because one acted as the stop for the outer cable and the other connected to the inner.

Due to this the cams did not move the shoes by equal amounts, and in later years owners found that longer levers and careful setting up were needed to get the brake to work well.

There were new air filters and side panels to suit the new frame, and further style came from the silencers. For the road models these became of megaphone form, mounted one on each side low down, but the TR6C maintained its past style. Thus, both pipes curled round to waist level on the left where they were joined by a balance pipe and to twin silencers. The model was also alone in having an undershield and folding footrests plus a smaller headlight and only a speedometer, while the others had a rev counter as well.

The major change to the engine during 1972 was to the cylinder head, beginning with engine number XG42304. The new part had push-in exhaust pipes in place of the long-established arrangement of thread-

By 1973 the larger Bonneville had a disc front brake and was also offered in street-scrambler form as this TR7RV. It has one carburettor, and the letter V in the name indicates a five-speed gearbox.

ed ports, screwed-in adapters and clamped-on pipes. At the same time, the inlet side of the twin-carburettor head was amended to accept mounting blocks on studs in place of the old ones which screwed in and were locked with a large nut. To go with all this, there were new rocker boxes, each with a single flat access lid in place of the familiar inspection caps so often lost during a journey.

All models were offered with a five-speed gearbox for 1972 and this, as a complete assembly, went into the same shell as the four-speed type. To distinguish the model, a letter V was added to the reference. In most other respects the machines were as for 1971, although modifications had been made to reduce the seat height.

The major news for 1973 was of two larger models, at first of 725 cc and later 744 cc. These were the T140V and TR7V, also listed as the T140RV and TR7RV in USA form. Both had engines bored out to increase the capacity and a new cylinder head

with ten fixings, but otherwise continued in the Triumph mould of before.

The new 750s were listed only with five speeds and went into the common set of cycle parts. There was a noticeable change at the front end with the appearance of a single disc brake and new headlamp brackets, which were much more in the older style, and for the home market there were gaiters as well. The disc went on the left of the hub and had hydraulic operation, with its master cylinder clamped to the handlebar.

One unfortunate side effect of the greater capacity was an increase in vibration, and Edward Turner had always held that 650 cc and 6500 rpm were about the limit for a parallel twin without balance shafts. The new models exceeded both figures, so the problem became more acute when the rider used all the performance to keep up with some of the new, big Japanese fours which had arrived.

There was one oddity in 1973, this being the BSA T65 Thunderbolt. This was a fac-

The T140V Bonneville for the USA in 1973 with raised bars and a small petrol tank as demanded by that market. The engine has the ten-stud head used by the 744 cc models, and mixes the old Triumph lines with its unit construction.

tory Tribsa, a batch of 264 machines built for an overseas customer in August 1972, mainly from Triumph parts. In essence they were the TR6 model with BSA badges and markings on the tank and side panels. In most respects the machines were strictly to the 1972 standard, but differed in having the 1969-70 type of twin-leading-shoe front brake and full-width hub fitted into the 1973 front forks complete with gaiters.

At the end of the year the TR6 and four-speed T120 models were dropped, and from September 1973 the work force barricaded the factory gates and began the eighteen-month sit-in. During that time few machines left Meriden, but they did include the last of the T120V models.

The only obvious change on the 1974 models was to new silencers with slow-taper, reverse cone ends. A few machines of both capacities were released from the works during the year, but the remainder of the 1974 output did not leave until March to May 1975, after the blockade was over.

By then the factory situation was totally changed following two general elections and the formation of a Labour government. With left-winger Tony Benn now involved in the industrial scene, the notion the work force had suggested of a co-operative became a real possibility. Negotiations dragged on for some time, but early in 1975 it came into being and in time became Meriden Motorcycles Limited.

Prospects

Despite the many models, it is three stars for the TR6 and four for the T120 and T140. The latter is invariably the preferred model and fetches the better price, although the Trophy is the machine normally used by regular riders.

The models are split into those with the 1971-on frame and the older types, with the latter maybe having a small edge. Also, some versions may be more preferred than others or may be harder to find. In the main, these are slight variations and depend on local conditions and market demand.

The Thunderbird is also a middle-of-the-road three-star model that keeps up with the times but no more. The single exception is

the 1966 version which lacks the skirt so has something less in its favour and drops to two stars. If you want a machine with a nacelle, the earlier ones are more likely to appreciate and thus remain a better bet.

Thus the Bonneville remains the best option for investment and performance, while the Trophy continues to offer less need for maintenance in daily use.

The Thruxton Bonneville is a five-star bike if it is genuine. These are rare bikes and few have survived intact.

US Variants

When the 649 cc unit-construction range was introduced for 1963 there were two variants of the TR6 for the USA. These were the Highway Trophy TR6S/R, which was essentially the home-market model fitted with high bars and twin silencers. For off-road use there was the TR6S/C with an open, waist-level exhaust pipe running along each side, no lights and trail tyres.

Fuel tanks for both TR6 models were smaller than for the UK but the finish remained in Regal purple and silver. For even more performance the machine was offered on the West Coast in twin-carburettor form as the T120TT, running a 12:1 compression ratio.

The two TR6 models ran on as they were for 1964 with the general range changes but in sapphire red and silver. The T120TT became the T120C in gold and white. For 1965 it was the same, the finishes changing to gold and white for the TR models, and blue and silver for the T120C. After this the TR6R and TR6C general export models replaced them to run on to the end of the 649 cc twins.

A further rare US model appeared in 1970, this being the T120RT, which was only sold after the customer had signed away all his warranty rights. It was also not the normal 649 cc expected of a T120, but of 744 cc as was to come with the T140, and built for racing.

The races it was intended for were the AMA series of 1970, the first year that allowed all 750 cc machines to compete, regardless of their valve location. To take part, machines had to be homologated which meant producing a batch of 200.

For this, the Bonneville engine was bored out to 76 mm and 744 cc, this being feasible with the stock block, even if on the limit. Further tuning pushed up the power enough for Gene Romero to win the Number One plate in 1970, coming close to retaining it for 1971.

The model was not mentioned in its home country and its short existence was soon forgotten. The small number of machines actually prepared and raced continued in use during the early 1970s while the remainder of the 200 found homes and were often seen as stock T120 Bonnevilles that happened to run faster than usual. One or two eventually returned to Britain, imported privately many years later.

Prospects

Four stars for the TR6 machines, five for the T120 models for these are rare and interesting. Few will have remained standard over the year so one such could be a nice find, especially in its home country.

Chapter 4

Meriden and Devon big twins

★★	**Daytona 600 1983**
★★	**Thunderbird 600 1983**
★★	**TR65 Thunderbird 1981-82**
★★	**TR65T Tiger Trail 1982**
★★★	**TR7V Tiger 1976-81**
★★	**TR7T Tiger Trail 1981-82**
★★★	**T140V Bonneville 1976-78**
★★★★	**Silver Jubilee Bonneville 1977**
★★★★	**T140D Bonneville Special 1979-80**
★★★	**T140E Bonneville 1978-82**
★★★	**T140ES Bonneville Electro 1980-83**
★★★★	**Executive Bonneville 1980-82**
★★★★	**Royal Bonneville 1981**
★★★	**TSS 1982-83**
★★★	**TSS A/V 1983**
★★★	**TSX 1982-83**
★★	**Devon Bonneville 1985-88**

Meriden was not the only co-operative set up by Tony Benn in 1975 but it was to last the longest and had the best chance of success. The workforce had a real interest and enthusiasm for motorcycles so the product had every reason to be well made, correctly assembled and fully tested before going out to the customer.

If the socialist dream was to work it should have succeeded at Meriden, but many factors were to make the workforce's task harder. Triumph's financial background was complex, and with cash flow a continual critical factor they found themselves facing a crisis about once a year. Most times this resulted in a cut in the work force.

There were also technical problems to solve for emission legislation, especially in the all-important American market, which meant long and expensive tests. By the time these had been complied with there was little time or money left for future development.

Not that they did not try. They had their success later in the decade, for enthusiasm for the simple Triumph continued among a sea of Japanese fours. Industrial conditions in England sank low at that time but were not a problem at Meriden, although they may have suffered from the troubles of others. For all that the workforce entered the 1980s still going strong.

Meriden models

The first Meriden co-operative machine was built in April 1975, and up to June that year they built T140 models in the 1974 form. The switch was then made to the new 1976 specification, and this was distinguished from the older one by a left-side gearchange lever and a disc brake for the rear wheel. Two models were listed as the Tiger TR7V and Bonneville T140V with one or two carburettors respectively. Otherwise they were the same machine with the five-speed, 744 cc engine unit.

Both ran on into 1977 with no changes when they were joined by the Silver Jubilee Bonneville. In celebration of the Queen's jubilee, the model had a special finish in red, white and blue on silver, and there was more chrome and polish than usual. One thousand of these models went to the United Kingdom and the United States each, with 400 going to other countries, each with a certificate of origin.

It was back to the two-model range for 1978 with a halogen headlight bulb and new dual seat. For the United States, the Bonneville became the T140E with Concentric Mk II carburettors and revised engine breathing in order to cope with the emission control regulations. For this there was a new cylinder head with parallel inlet ports which allowed the use of a common choke lever for both Amals.

The T140E replaced the earlier model on the home market for 1979, and both it and the TR7V were given electronic ignition, neutral light and a rear carrier. Both machines were built in UK and USA specifications, but the differences were small and mainly concerned gas tanks and bars.

During the year a further model was introduced as the T140D Bonneville Special, which had cast alloy Lester wheels, two-into-one exhaust with the silencer low down on the right, a stepped seat and high bars. It also had the rear brake caliper mounted above the wheel centre, unlike the other models, but they were changed to match for 1980. That year all engines had an improved

This 1978 T140 Bonneville has high bars for the American market and a disc brake for the rear wheel. Its pedal is now on the right and the gear pedal has moved to the left to conform with the needs of the times.

The Silver Jubilee model was a limited edition Bonneville built in 1977 to celebrate the Queen's anniversary. It had Red Arrow tyres and Girling gas shocks as standard and a rather special finish. This gave it more chrome and polish than usual, and the paintwork was naturally in red, white and blue. This one has had a fairing added.

oil pump with four valves and an exhaust system that was tucked in farther.

An optional electric start for the T140E was announced early in the year but did not get into production until May. The starter motor went in the old magneto position behind the block and drove the crankshaft via the timing gear train to make a neat and effective assembly. The resultant machine was listed as the T140ES.

It was joined, in July 1980, by the Executive Bonneville which was sold with a Sabre cockpit fairing, by Brealey-Smith, and panniers and top box by Sigma. The machine was given a custom paint finish in deep maroon shading to ruby with gold lining and was shown to press and public at the Tourist Trophy that year. It made a handsome machine.

The Executive Bonneville performed in the manner expected of a Triumph from that decade. The low-speed vibration made

the forks twitch as the machine sat at tickover, but smoothed out as soon as the clutch went home. The sheer grunt was still there, as was the nice gearbox, so the rider could be brisk or laid-back as the mood took and the machine would respond well.

By then the Bonneville was far outclassed in sheer performance. The same speed could be had from far fewer Japanese cubic centimetres but of course their style of delivery was totally different. The Triumph offered its own style of motorcycling which a good many riders continued to appreciate and prefer.

The electric start became an option for all 1981 models, along with the siamesed exhaust and alloy wheels from the T140D, although the wheels were now by Morris as the Lesters became hard to get. The exhaust pipes were clamped into the ports instead of simply pushing in, and there were a number of detail improvements.

At the August 1980 show, where the 1981 model range was first shown, Triumph also had a project machine to test public reaction. This was called the T140PE Phoenix and was

The T140D Special appeared in 1979 with a number of special features. Notable were the Lester cast alloy wheels and the two-into-one exhaust system with single silencer. There is also a stepped seat and high bars to fit in with the custom-type style.

The T140E model appeared for 1978 for the USA with improved Amal Concentric carburettors and breathing to help it meet the emission requirements. It had parallel inlet ports and for 1979 gained electronic ignition. This one is from 1980 and was a prize in a show competition and thus a little more special in its finish.

in the chopper or custom mould, with Low-boy styling achieved with extended forks, longer rear fork, laid-down shocks and a stepped seat. A narrow 3.00 in. tyre went on the front with a fat 5.10x16 in. at the rear. The engine was the T140E but with the older splayed head, although the Mk II Concentrics were retained.

Later in the year the factory learned that most of their debt to the government was to be wiped out, and around that time the co-operative became a limited company with directors while the workers became the shareholders.

This persuaded Triumph to introduce the TR7T Tiger Trail model at the Paris show. This was more in the style of the old Trophy. The engine was detuned by changing the pistons and inlet camshaft but was otherwise the faithful, single-carburettor 744 cc unit. The frame was stock but the forks had gaiters and carried a 21 in. front wheel and a sprung trials plastic mudguard. The front

The T140 Executive model was another introduced in 1980 and came with Sabre cockpit fairing and Sigma panniers as well as the electric start of the T140ES it was based on. This example was owned by Mike Thompson, the owner's club chairman of that year.

The T140ES with electric starter was first offered in 1980 and was based on the T140E model. The rear caliper is above the disc, and later models had further options of exhaust system and cast alloy Morris wheels with dual discs at the front. This one just has some added luggage equipment.

The Thunderbird name was revived in 1981 for this TR65 model. It used a 649 cc short-stroke version of the Triumph engine with single carburettor, and was a low-cost machine. To keep the price low there was a drum rear brake, points ignition and a matt-black finish for engine and exhaust system.

brake remained a disc but the rear was a drum revised to suit the right-side pedal, and both wheels had trail tyres fitted.

The exhausts were siamesed to a silencer on the left which was waist level on the prototype but ran up at an angle from a low pipe in production. They were finished in matt black which contrasted well with the yellow used for the tank, mudguards and side panels. A short dual seat was used along with an undershield, braced bars and a minimum of plating.

Behind the scenes Triumph had been at work on an antivibration engine mounting. The original design was done by Bernard Hooper along the lines of his successful Norton Commando, so the whole engine and gearbox unit became rubber mounted and

The 1981 TR7T Tiger Trail was introduced at the Paris show as a modern version of the old Trophy model for off-road riding. It appeared

with more than one style of exhaust system and had a detuned engine in a stock frame, with wheels to suit its job.

able to move up and down within limits. These were imposed by rubber blocks above and below the engine and the rear engine plates which carried the pivot for the rear fork. Just below this went a second cross-shaft attached to lugs on the frame, and links connected the two pivots. This meant that the engine unit and rear fork kept in line and could rock about the lower pivot or move fore and aft to a limited extent.

The antivibration mounts were first tried out on some machines supplied to the police, as this ensured a good feedback on how they performed. The machines themselves were Bonnevilles fitted with the usual fairing, panniers and police equipment plus twin discs at the front to keep the weight under control.

In April 1981 there was another show and Triumph used it to launch a new model with an old name, the TR65 Thunderbird. This was of 649 cc, and the capacity reduction

In April 1981 the TS8-1 was shown to the public and had the eight-valve, all-alloy engine with antivibration mountings. The styling was by Ian Dyson and featured a special fairing with twin headlights and unusual lines.

came from reducing the stroke which meant a new crankshaft and shorter block. It was a cost-conscious model so kept to one carbu-

The 1981 Bonneville T140 Royal was a limited edition celebrating the wedding of Prince Charles and Lady Di. It was built in two forms, with this the United Kingdom version with Mor-

ris cast wheels and dual discs at the front. For the United States it had wire wheels and one disc. Both had Bing carburettors.

rettor, a drum rear brake, points ignition and a matt-black engine finish. The exhaust system was siamesed to a silencer low on the left and this too was all in matt black.

The T140D was dropped, since the same result could be built using the option list. This extended to twin front discs for the T140E or the Executive, along with the alloy wheels. The cockpit fairing was offered as an option for the T140E while remaining standard for the Executive, for which a full fairing became an option. The T140E continued to be listed in electric-start form and all models were available in a USA style, while the TR7V ran on to the middle of the year. The Executive alone was fitted with twin Bing constant-vacuum carburettors in place of the usual Amals.

Also at the April show was the TS8-1, which had an eight-valve engine and a fair-

Triumph sales manager Alastair Ritchie on the T140TSS at its launch in Kensington, London, in 1982. It had the eight-valve, all-alloy engine fed by twin Amal carburettors, and options of cast wheels and antivibration engine mounts.

ing with twin headlights and rather unusual lines styled by Ian Dyson. The engine had an alloy block and sat in the antivibration mounts, while inside it there was a stronger crankshaft. The carburettors were Bing and the machine was finished in black.

In the middle of the year Triumph produced another royal special, this time to celebrate the wedding of Prince Charles to Lady Di. Only 250 were made for the UK market, and both home and USA models were produced. All were based on the T140ES but with the Bing carburettors. The USA version had wire wheels and one front disc, while the UK had the Morris alloy wheels and dual discs.

Near the end of 1981 a 649 cc version of the Tiger Trail was announced and ran alongside the TR7T. The smaller machine followed the lines of the larger except it lacked electronic ignition, while its road equivalent, the TR65 Thunderbird, changed to the standard exhaust system and paint job for 1982, with the option of twin front discs for its wire-spoked front wheel.

The various T140 models continued for 1982, all with wire wheels as standard and the cast ones as an option along with twin front discs. The base model continued to have the electric start as an option.

There were two new models, with the TSS having the eight-valve engine and antivibration mounting and the TSX a custom style on the stock T140. The TSS engine was similar to the TS8-1 with alloy top half and Amal carburettors, but inside had a strengthened crankshaft with larger big-end bearings. On the cycle side the TSS no longer had the special fairing but came in normal T140 cycle parts including the stock frame, although the rear fork was controlled by Marzocchi units. The wheels had wire spokes, but twin front discs were fitted while the cast wheels were an option.

The TSX was the T140 with Bing carburettors but in custom form, with 16 in. rear wheel, two-level seat and high bars. The twin front discs remained an option while both wheels were cast alloy as standard. It featured plain megaphone silencers and a custom paint job. Toward the end of 1982 the Tiger Trail models were dropped, since only about 250 had been sold, mainly in Europe.

The firm exhibited an all-new, twin-cylinder, water-cooled prototype early in 1983 both as an engine and a complete machine. The engine had chain-driven twin overhead camshafts to operate its eight valves, and four separate exhaust ports and pipes. Inside there was a short stroke and a balancing device to cut down vibration.

The machine was kept up on a pedestal out of harm's way and was one of several design studies. It had conventional modern lines for the time, with the engine a stressed member of the frame and monoshock rear suspension, telescopic front forks, cast wheels and disc brakes on both wheels. It carried the name Phoenix 900 and the engine was coded Diana.

At the same show the firm launched a new pair of models as the Thunderbird 600 and Daytona 600, with a 599 cc engine produced by further shortening of the stroke. The two were similar, although they had one and two carburettors respectively, and the first was in a custom style with 16 in. rear wheel and two-level seat. Both had wire wheels, single front disc, with the twin discs as an option, drum rear brake and many common parts. The Daytona had the larger petrol tank and also a tail fairing to the seat.

This seat tail also went on the home market T140ES, while the version for the United States mirrored the Thunderbird except in having twin carburettors. The same variation distinguished the TSS and TSX models, with the latter in the United States style and retaining its cast alloy wheels. It was listed in two forms, with the TSX4 using the normal engine and the TSX8 the eight-valve version although at a lower compression ratio.

The TSS model was also available in two forms, but in this case with either the standard frame or the frame with antivibration mountings. The cast alloy wheels continued to be an option, and none of the range had a kickstart, so all relied on their electric foot.

All this proved to be a desperate last attempt for the workforce; by the middle of the year they ran out of money. In August Triumph decided to call in the liquidator, and

near the end of the year the plant, machines and factory were auctioned. Soon afterward the famous Triumph factory was demolished.

Devon models

That should have been the end, but as it turned out, it was not. The manufacturing rights were bought by businessman John Bloor, who licensed Racing Spares to produce the Bonneville for five years. That firm

The custom-styled T140TSX of 1982 with its cast wheels, 16 in. at the rear, two-level seat and high bars. Megaphone silencers were fitted and dual front discs an option. Not a bad idea to exploit a further section of the market, although Triumph days at Meriden were then numbered.

The Phoenix 900 water-cooled twin was shown early in 1983 but kept up on its plinth during the show to avoid too close an inspection. There was also a development engine with test rig mountings to be seen, but few details were divulged.

was run by Les Harris who had been making Triumph, BSA and Norton spares for twenty years at a factory in Bedfordshire and had, paradoxically, been heartily condemned by the Meriden workforce for taking profitable spares business from them. However, it did leave him in the best position to move on from parts to complete machines.

While Harris began to organize a production line at a factory in Devon, Bloor ensured that the machines being built were totally in the old Bonneville mould. This left him free to plan a modern factory on a green-field site where he proposed to build a new Triumph multi. This took some years to develop, but by 1988 there were reports of a one-litre, four-cylinder, water-cooled engine in existence. Twin overhead camshafts were mentioned and the unit was on trial in a chassis from one of the top English frame-building firms.

Meanwhile, Harris set up his line and organized his supplies. Many of these came from Europe, for the demise of the English

motorcycle industry had caused nearly all the supply firms to move to other fields. Thus the brakes were Brembo, the forks Paioli and the instruments Veglia.

The Devon Bonnevilles did not reach the market until the middle of 1985 and were much as in the past. There were two model builds, one for the home market and another for the United States, but the differences were essentially the fuel tank and handlebars. The finish was in black with gold line or a red flash for either, with the black extending to the lower fork legs as well as the frame and side covers.

The engine was the tried and true 744 cc unit, but many of its component parts were made on computer-controlled machines. This gave far greater accuracy than had ever been possible at Meriden and played its part in making the engines oil-tight and quiet. They looked just the same as before and retained their lines which were approaching the half century.

The transmission continued with five speeds but there was no electric starter, just the old-fashioned lever for the foot. The carburettors were Mk 1½ Amal Concentrics which were in effect the original instrument fitted with the Mk II cold-start system. Their use cured an annoying hesitation on acceleration.

The cycle side remained basically as it had been at Meriden, even though much of it came from abroad. The frame still had duplex downtubes and carried the engine oil in its top and seat tubes, while the rear fork was controlled by twin shock absorbers. Slimline forks went at the front, and the wheels had wire spokes with twin discs on the 19 in. front and a single disc for the 18 in. rear.

The new machines had a favourable reception and continued with the easy handling and good mid-range torque of old. The footrests were still too far forward for real comfort at speed, but their position was dictated by the need for the gear lever shaft to run across ahead of the clutch. For serious work a rearset kit was an advantage on any model with left-foot gearchange, although high-speed motorway cruising was not really what the machine was all about.

In the end the Bonneville did not get back into the United States, but this had nothing to do with meeting emission limits or the fact that Les Harris did not wish to sell there. The reason was the need for two lots of very expensive product liability insurance to cover both his company and John Bloor. The premium for this was such that it made the machine uneconomical to sell in the United States. So thanks to the dealings of lawyers, the Americans had to go without.

Other problems came to the surface during 1988 when it became necessary to order a large batch of crankcases. This considerable investment came at a point when the agreement to make the machine was close to its end and even more stringent emission regulations were appearing on the horizon.

The firm had by then revived the Matchless name for a 500 cc single which used a Rotax engine, and it made sense to concentrate on this. The costs of the parts and the query over the continuance of the license made this the sensible commercial decision to make, so the Bonneville was once again laid to rest as it had been so often in the past. Whether it will make another Phoenix-style entrance or whether the Bloor project will become production machines on the showroom floor, only time will tell.

Prospects

The big twins generally rate lower than the older models, as collectors invariably prefer old to new, but possible exceptions are the more specialized or short-run machines. Thus mainly three stars are awarded, along with a few twos or fours, although the machines are less easy to judge than for most other years and ranges.

The 600s and 650s are down to two stars along with the trail models, as they are

Another attempt to keep the firm in business resulted in this Daytona 600 of 1983, which was joined by a custom version listed as the Thunderbird 600. The reduced capacity allowed them to be in a cheaper insurance category which was to be the incentive to buy. Few did.

After Meriden closed, the Bonneville was built in Devon by Les Harris, under license from 1985-88. It still had the lines as laid down by Edward Turner in 1937, but many parts now came from other countries. It was received well and continued to offer the same easy riding as in the past.

simply less desirable than the 750s. Nice machines maybe—but not the choice of many. The same applies to the post-Meriden machines from Devon, for they are too new for most people.

Four stars go to the Jubilee and Royal but only if in fully original condition. The same applies for the T140D and the Executive. The first of these was not quite mainline so could be collectible, while the second was a nice motorcycle.

Despite all this, rating is still a subjective area and more likely to alter dramatically over the years. For investors, these models are more of a gamble, but less so for riders if you can find a good, clean example that has been fully sorted.

★★★★★	T150 Trident 1968-70
★★★★	T150 Trident 1971-72
★★★★★	T150V Trident 1972-74
★★★★	X75 Hurricane 1973
★★★★	TI60V Trident 1975-76

Trident

The idea of a three-cylinder Triumph was first aired early in the 1960s, but it was some years before even the first prototype was built. It was 1968 when the machine was finally launched for export only, and the next year before it reached the home market.

The triple came in two forms, with vertical cylinders for the T150 Trident and inclined ones for the matching BSA Rocket 3. This difference had a considerable effect on the overall appearance of the two models and on some of the major engine castings, but did allow the Triumph to retain its own engine style.

The three-cylinder power unit was based heavily on the Triumph twin and was known at one time as a Tiger one-and-a-half. The construction resulted in parts that were complex and expensive to make because it remained much as the prototype, which had used twin parts adapted or added to for convenience. In this form it was not really intended for production, but once the decision to go ahead was made there was no time to start with a clean sheet of paper.

Triples

The triple was built with a three-part crankcase that was expensive and difficult to machine. The two outer parts were similar to the case halves of a twin, and each had camshaft bushes fore and aft of the cylinder in the Triumph manner. Neither extended back to the gearbox but did run back enough

One of the first 1968 T150 Trident machines being handed over for a road test. Original features were the ray gun silencers with their triple outlets and early twin-leading-shoe, drum front brake. A fine, fast motorcycle much in the English tradition.

to house the oil pump in the left case and a filter in the right, this running across to the left via the centre casting.

This centre acted as a massive distance piece between the two outers and was extended to enclose the gearbox. It was open at the top to allow the crankshaft to be fitted, and this went into two split housings with shell bearings. The centre case thus served the middle cylinder, but the bolted-up assembly lacked the basic structural strength that would have come if the horizontal case joint favoured by most modern multis had been used.

Inside the case went a one-piece crankshaft supported by its two plain centre mains, and drive-side ball and timing-side roller races. Alloy rods with plain big-end

shells were used and the gudgeon pins ran direct in their small ends.

The pistons they carried moved in a one-piece cylinder block cast in light alloy with pressed-in liners. The usual Triumph tappet guide block went between each cylinder pair, but the left ones had only one tappet fitted to them. The pushrod tubes were stock Triumph parts and above them went the one-piece light alloy cylinder head. This was built in the Meriden style, with separate rocker boxes, each which contained three rockers, a spindle and a variety of washers and spacers. Lubrication was by a feed to the spindle ends and access via a long cover on each box, both of which were finned.

The exhaust ports had adapters screwed into them with a built-up manifold on the

A Trident pictured with many BSA sporting personalities who are about to leave for the United States in 1970. The machine now has the later type of front brake and has lost the lower rear unit covers, but is otherwise little changed.

inlet side. A stub was bolted to each inlet port and connected by a short length of rubber hose to a common manifold casting. This carried the throttle linkage and all three Amal Concentric carburettors.

The timing side was pure Triumph, with a train of gears to drive the two camshafts. The exhaust one drove the points cam from its right end, so the timing cover carried the points themselves under a small cover while the rev counter was skew-gear driven from the middle of the camshaft. Features that were moved from their normal Triumph

twin position were the alternator, which went in the timing chest, and the oil pump. This was fitted low down in the left crankcase, where it was driven from the crankshaft by gears located in the primary chaincase. Lubrication was dry sump with an external oil tank, and the system included an oil cooler which went under the front of the petrol tank.

The gearbox was stock four-speed Triumph as used by the larger twins, but the clutch was not. To deal with the power, a diaphragm Borg & Beck unit with single

For 1971 the Trident lost its ray gun silencers and came with conventional megaphone ones. It was also fitted with the group slimline forks and conical hubs, with ineffective front brake.

The twin-leading-shoes were hardly up to stopping the weight or speed of this quick motorcycle.

plate was fitted, with its release mechanism outboard of it in the primary chaincase outer. It was driven by a triplex roller chain and this tensioned by a pair of slipper blades.

The chaincase had an inner and outer casting and a clutch cover went between the inner and the gearbox. Thus the clutch ran dry and inboard of the chain with the final-drive sprocket further in still.

The cycle parts came mainly from the 650 twins, so the frame had single top, down and seat tubes with splayed-out duplex rails under the engine unit. The subframe was bolted in place and the rear fork pivoted in the same way from the same lug, with limited bracing provided by the rear engine plates.

The front forks were the normal Triumph components complete with friction steering damper. The front wheel had the full-width hub with the 8 in. twin-leading-shoe brake, with the extended front cam lever and the operating cable sweeping in from the rear. For the rear wheel there was the usual offset

hub with 7 in. brake drum as used by the twins.

The machine's distinct looks came partly from the oil cooler already mentioned and from a slab-sided petrol tank. The exhaust system also had some special features, as it went three into four into two. This was done with the manifold, in which the centre pipe was split into two, each side run into an outer pipe which then ran back to the silencers. These were of a flattened oval section, tapering out as they ran back and cut off at an angle at the rear. The ends were blanked-off by flat plates and each carried three short outlet stubs. They were quickly known as "ray gun" silencers.

The oil tank went on the right under the hinged seat nose, with the battery beside it. Side covers kept them and the toolbox out of sight and also enclosed the massive air filter. Most of the fixtures and fittings were similar to those found on the twins, but the instruments did go into a binnacle at the top of the forks.

For 1972 the Trident gained five speeds during the year to become the T150V. Unfortunately it had to wait until the next year for a disc brake to replace the overstressed drum when it was also given fork gaiters once more.

The result was a fine motorcycle, although it was not helped in some markets by the styling it had been given or the point in time when it was launched. In October 1968 the Honda CB750 appeared, and upstaged the Trident with its overhead camshaft, five speeds, electric start and disc front brake. Most of all, the Honda was available in large numbers worldwide. Never before had this happened with a four-cylinder road motorcycle.

On the road, the Trident was as fast in a straight line as the Honda and handled much better, but only the enthusiasts knew this. Far more people put their money down on the Honda for its features and style, never to ride it hard enough to realize its limitations.

The Trident sold only moderately well and was released onto its home market early in 1969. By this time the front brake had been altered to the bell-crank lever type with appropriate change of backplate, and the machine continued into 1970 with detail improvements and the loss of the rear suspension unit lower covers.

The cycle side was revised much more for 1971 in line with the changes on the larger twins but did retain its frame. This was fitted with the slimline front forks with four-stud cap fixing and no gaiters. Into them went the conical hub with 8 in. twin-leading shoe brake, and the rear hub also changed to the conical type. The rear units lost the rest of their covers and the silencers were changed to the shallow megaphone style used by the twins. Turn signals and side reflectors were added.

The engine unit had not been altered for 1971 and stayed that way until mid-1972, when a five-speed gearbox was fitted creating the T150V. The box could go into the earlier engine units provided all the parts were changed.

The machine began the 1973 season in this form but it had barely got under way before the front brake was changed to a 10 in. disc with hydraulic operation. At the same time gaiters reappeared on the front forks which gave the oil seals an easier time.

For 1973 the Trident was joined by the X75 Hurricane which was derived from it and styled by Craig Vetter. It leaned to the

The X75 Hurricane version of the Trident was based on the inclined triple engine used by the BSA Rocket and later Trident T160. It had its own special style set off by the three pipes on the right and kept the conical hub at the front. Interesting but short-lived.

chopper form with extended forks and longer wheelbase but not to any extreme. It differed from the Trident in using the BSA engine with inclined cylinders, and had this slotted into the BSA frame. The oddest feature was the exhaust; all three pipes ran separately to the right of the machine where three short megaphone-style silencers sat one above the other. The left side ended up looking rather bare and is rarely photographed, but access to the chain case is first class.

Unlike the Trident, the X75 stuck with the conical hub and drum brake while the wheels had skimpy mudguards. The styling was topped by a one-piece glass fibre moulding that enclosed the steel tank and flowed back to form side covers and the seat base.

The seat itself was short, and high-rise bars were fitted, since it was a model for boulevard cruising rather than fast riding. An unusual feature was the fitting of light alloy wheel rims, but most of the finish was chrome with a red paint job plus yellow stripes for the glass fibre moulding.

The Hurricane was built only for that one year, which finished with the factory sit-in and the movement of all triple production to the BSA factory at Small Heath. With all the trauma this caused, the machines continued as they were.

It was not until 1975 that changes came, and when they did they were fairly major. The engine became the BSA type with inclined cylinders but amended around the timing and gearbox end covers to retain the Triumph line. Internally it was much as before, although the primary chain became a duplex type and the rev-counter drive was taken from the left end of the exhaust camshaft. On the outside, an electric starter appeared and the exhaust system was revised with four pipes leading down to two long silencers. This was done with an alloy

This Trident with disc front brake was a prize in a Bike British Bonanza competition around 1973. It thus has the five speeds of the T150V, fork gaiters and a fine turn of speed with good handling.

adapter in the central cylinder port and a junction between each pair of pipes under the engine.

The gearbox kept its five speeds but the gear pedal moved over to the left so the brake had to go over to the right. Its change was matched at the rear wheel where a 10 in. disc was fitted and the two were linked by hydraulic operation.

The model was known as the T160V, but time was running out for it and early in 1976 the last one left the production line. This should have been the end and for the factory model it was, but the Trident was to continue in special, small numbers.

This was due to the efforts of Les Williams who had worked at Meriden and later went into business for himself selling standard spares and special parts for Tridents and

From 1975 the Trident was listed as the T160 and fitted with the inclined engine but amended to keep the Triumph line. It had a disc rear brake and electric starter and is here seen in police form, which could catch most culprits.

Drive side of the T160 which had a duplex primary chain and rev counter drive from the left end of the exhaust camshaft. The exhaust system became three into four into two, and the gear pedal has moved over to the left.

other models. Eventually this work led to developing complete motorcycles.

Williams was race shop manager in the early 1970s when the works racing triples had their many successes. He became associated with one model in particular which was called *Slippery Sam* after major oil leaks during the 1970 Bol d'Or. In 1971 this machine ran in the production TT for the second time and won it. For 1972 Williams prepared it at home for the same race and it won a second time. After that, Williams bought the triple and it went on to win for three more years to bring its total to five consecutive wins, after which it went into retirement.

Following this, Williams set up his own shop and began to produce replicas of *Sam* using well-prepared T160V machines with some cosmetic changes. From this activity the Legend model was developed, which could well represent what the factory might have built for the mid-1980s.

The essentials remained the same, so the start of each Legend was a T160V. Each was built to a customer's requirements so variations were possible, but normally there were late-type forks, cast alloy wheels and twin

Three ladies with a triple T180 and other Triumphs, including a Hurricane to the right. This was no longer listed when the T180 appeared but was not a fast seller at the time. Now a rare model, so collectable, but the stock Trident was better on the road.

discs at the front. These modern features went well with the styling, which was from around 1980, in a nice restrained manner. The twin rear shocks were also of this time, as well as the side panels, a good-size tank and a seat base with a neat hump.

The handlebars were short and flat while the footrests were farther to the rear than usual. The result was a rather nice machine for covering large distances at speed. It made for a relaxed ride and easy handling, which made riding long distances a pleasure.

Production was, invariably, in small numbers but the machines were well worth owning by anyone wanting to travel far and fast—or slow—on a big Triumph.

Prospects

At least four stars awarded for any Trident triple, for they are among the classic motorcycles and possibly an even better investment than the Bonneville. The early T150s of 1968–70 could well rate a five, as they represent the Triumph marque before the major range changes for 1971 which introduced the slimline forks and conical hubs. These were not to everyone's taste, however.

The T150V of 1972–74 could also rate five stars for being rare, especially the first machines with the drum brake in this instance. The later models, with front disc, were also thin on the ground due to the factory problems and could be quite desirable for riders seeking a triple with disc brake and right-side gear pedal.

The Legend should continue this high standard and as a highly desirable motorcycle rates four stars minimum. It could rise to five in view of the small numbers in existence, since it is a machine bought for actual use so rarely comes onto the market. Owners tend to keep them for high days and fast riding in the true Trident tradition.

The Trident is truly one of the best for both riding and investment.

Chapter 6

Singles

★★★	2H 1937-40
★★★	2HC 1938-39
★★★★	T70 Tiger 70 1936-40
★★★★★	T70 Competition 1937-39
★★	3S 1937-40
★★	3SC 1938-39
★★	3SE 1940
★★★	3H 1937-40
★★★★	T80 Tiger 80 1936-40
★★★★★	T80 Competition 1937-39
★★	5S 1939-40
★★	5SE 1940
★★★	5H 1937-39
★★★★	T90 Tiger 90 1936-38
★★★★★	T90 Competition 1937-38
★★	6S 1937-40
★★★	T15 Terrier 1953-56
★★★	T20 Tiger Cub 1954-56
★★	T20 Tiger Cub 1957-62
★	T20 Tiger Cub 1963-65
★	T20 Bantam Cub 1966
★	T20S/C Super Cub 1967-68
★★	T20S Sports Cub 1960
★★	T20S/L Sports Cub 1961
★★★	T20S/S Sports Cub 1962
★★	T20S/S Sports Cub 1963-66
★★★	T20S/H Sports Cub 1962
★★	T20S/H Sports Cub 1963-66
★★★	T20C Competiton Cub 1957-59
★★★	T20T Trials Cub 1961
★★★	TR20 Trials Cub 1962
★★	TR20 Trials Cub 1963-64
★	TR20 Trials Cub 1965-66
★★★	TS20 Scrambles Cub 1962
★★	TS20 Scrambles Cub 1963-64
★★	T20SM Mountain Cub 1965-66
★★	TR25W Trophy 1968-70
★★	T25SS Blazer SS 1971
★★	T25T Trail Blazer 1971
★★	TR5MX Avenger 1973-74

Triumph built a range of singles in the early thirties that ran from a 148 cc two-stroke to a 549 cc side-valve. These came with vertical or inclined cylinders to suit the whims of fashion. By 1934 some of these singles had been redesigned by Val Page, and while solid and dependable they lacked glamour and style.

This situation continued until 1936 when the firm changed hands and Edward Turner became its general manager. Within a few weeks he had the stylish Tiger models in the line-up, and for the next few years the list of models was arranged around the basic Page designs in forms that remained in use up to the war. Some continued in khaki for the duration.

The postwar range announced in March 1945 did include one single which was, in effect, the wartime 343 cc ohv model in a civilian black finish in place of khaki. It retained the girder forks and the basic Val Page all-iron engine with the usual Triumph four-speed gearbox, rigid frame and tank top instrument panel.

In the end this single was never produced postwar, as it made much more sense for the firm to concentrate on its twins while the surplus market was well stocked with ex-War Department Triumph singles, some of which were modified and did sterling duty in scrambles and grass-track events for a number of years.

Fresh postwar singles did not appear until the Terrier and Cub models came on the scene and they were aimed much more at the novice and commuter markets. From them was to come the BSA C15 series, and in time the wheel turned full circle and a version of the BSA led to a number of Triumph machines, including one expanded to a full 500 cc.

Prewar singles

When Turner arrived at Triumph he found that the bulk of the range was based on the

Happy couple with their cups among a sea of desirable machines, including the prewar Tiger single from 1939. It dates from the number plate surround, and shows the lines and finish that made the Tiger series so popular with riders of the times. The combination of chrome and silver sheen plus the Triumph lines proved a winner then and in the postwar years.

single-cylinder design laid down in 1934. He left it alone for the time being except for the sports versions, and for these he added style.

The results were the Tiger 70, 80 and 90 in 250, 350 and 500 cc capacities respectively. Their success came as much from the name as anything else. In addition to that they were given polished alloy cases, high-level exhausts and chrome-plated petrol tanks with silver sheen panels. The sparkle made all the difference and the machines sold well.

For 1937 there were major revisions to frames, forks and transmissions for all models, but the basic Page design remained. The engines all followed the same layout with a built-up crankshaft, vertically split alloy crankcase, and cast-iron head and barrel.

The timing side was on the right with a train of gears to the cams and then on to the mag-dyno, while the oil pump of the dry-sump system went on the timing case under its own cover.

The smallest engine was an ohv of 249 cc and was used by the 2H on which the Tiger 70 was based. Next came the 343 cc models, of which the 3S had side valves and the 3H and Tiger 80 were ohv. There were only ohv models in the 493 cc size and these were the 5H and Tiger 90, while the 598 cc 6S was the sole larger side-valve unit.

All these machines had much in common in terms of transmission and cycle parts, although the larger models had heavier components and the Tigers more chrome

A Smith illuminated Chronometric Trip Speedometer (80 m.p.h.)
will be supplied unless otherwise ordered, £2-10-0 extra.

The 1938 side-valve model 3S, which was also available as the 3SC with coil ignition. It was part of the model line-up of that period which were all based on one simple and sturdy design by Val Page, similar to those he produced for Ariel in the 1920s and for BSA for 1937.

and polish. There were also competition versions of these for trials use, with minor alterations to suit their intended use.

The range was successful with the public and for the company, thanks to its style and Triumph's commercial sense to produce a range from one basic layout. It continued

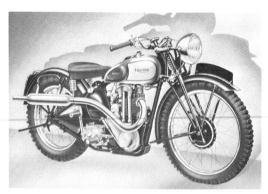

The competition Tiger model offered for 1938 in all three capacities. Each had a tuned engine and came with knobbly tyres, undershield, choice of gear ratios and increased ground clearance. Nice style and now rare.

into 1938 with two additions which had coil ignition in place of the usual magneto. These were the 249 cc 2HC and the 343 cc side-valve 3SC, both of which were reduced in price a little.

All ran on for 1939 except the Tiger 90 whose place was taken by the twin-cylinder T100. There was one new model in the shape of the 493 cc side-valve 5S which filled a small gap in the range and sold against other 500 cc side-valve singles.

The range announced for 1940 was curtailed a little and also altered. The competition Tigers were deleted, as were the 2HC and 5H. The Speed Twin took the place of the latter. The 3SC became the 3SE with trimmed specifications to reduce its price, and was joined by the 493 cc 5SE which followed the same lines but retained its magdyno. Both had an all-black finish and no instrument panel in the tank top, so used the small headlamp panel for the light switch and ammeter.

The other models remained in production but not for long. The firm turned to wartime versions of the singles, as detailed in the next chapter.

The touring ohv 3H of 1939, which was turned into the wartime single with integral rocker box. It was much as the other singles, all of which had many common parts, and served well in peace and war. Afterward, many were turned into competition machines for use in trials, scrambles, grass-track and road-racing events.

Prospects

Because of their age, all the ohv models must be three stars minimum and four stars for the Tiger models. I gave only two stars for the side-valve machines, although these could be pushing a three in the larger sizes.

A Smith illuminated Chronometric Trip Speedometer (120 m.p.h.) will be supplied unless otherwise ordered, £2-15-0 extra.

Top of the sporting models for 1938 was the Tiger 90 in its last year. It made a fine motorcycle for those times but the next year its place was taken by the new Tiger 100 twin, which backed up the 5T just as the sports singles backed the tourers and side-valve plodders.

The first small postwar single Triumph was the T15 Terrier seen here in 1954 form. From the start it had a plunger frame and the inimitable Triumph line to tank and nacelle, but also a weak big-end bearing which took far too long to sort out.

The competition versions of the Tiger models could rate five stars on rarity but only if totally genuine. Converted standard models would not make the grade, so it is important to be sure that it really is original.

All are likely to be good investments, more so the Tigers of course, but they are also nice machines to ride, easy to work on and some of the best of the old tradition. The handling may not be quite up to par, but with modern rubber compounds should be adequate for as much scratching as you would want to risk.

Terrier and Cubs

It was November 1952 before Triumph produced another single for the public and it was aimed at the commuter market, which they had rather ignored since 1939. Edward Turner held that the new model had to outperform its rivals, look like a Triumph and have enough sparkle so that any owner looking for a larger machine later on would keep to the Triumph marque.

The new machine was the T15 Terrier and stood out among a sea of two-strokes by dint of its overhead-valve engine. It did retain the Triumph line by copying the nacelle and tank badges of its larger brothers, and was built as a low-priced machine rather than a cheap bike. This gave the rider some real

The Terrier expanded into the larger 200 cc T20 Cub and at first used the same cycle parts including the plunger frame. This 1955 example was pictured much later, which explains the Hesketh in the background.

The basic Cub gained a pivoted fork frame for 1957 although the headstock support remained weak. This is the more sporting T20C intro- duced that year in an off-road style with wheels, tyres and undershield to suit but retaining the nacelle for the headlamp.

For 1959 the T20 Tiger Cub was fitted with a skirt similar to that used by later twins but with apertures for the oil tank and toolbox. The model now had a Zenith carburettor and a new tank badge but the big end was still a problem area.

The final year for the T20C was 1959 when it had deeper fins on the engine and the Zenith carburettor adopted the year before. It still kept the nacelle, but mudguards and other details remained to suit the off-road use.

benefits, and the extra cost was soon offset by lower fuel consumption and no need for petroil mixtures.

Sales manager Neale Shilton and publicity man Ivor Davies of Triumph with a prize winner—a T20—on the Triumph stand at an Earls Court show. All look pleased and no one is thinking about big-end life.

In this manner Turner avoided the use of a Villiers engine, as used by so many others, or having to design his own two-stroke, a field that would have been fresh ground to him and his team. It meant that they could use their four-stroke background and be reasonably sure that the design would need minimal development before it reached the public.

The Terrier engine had nearly square dimensions and a 149 cc capacity. It was built in unit with a four-speed gearbox and had the barrel inclined forward to be near parallel to the frame downtube, which resulted in nice clean lines for the complete assembly.

The engine was of conventional construction except that the vertical crankcase joint was moved over to the left of the crankshaft. This placed it on a line outboard of the final-drive sprocket, so that the left case cover was able to run straight back and form the inner primary chaincase clear of that sprocket. It did however mean that the crankcase joint had to be split to change the sprocket, and chain fitting was a nightmare unless a slave one was left in place.

Inside the crankcase the pressed-up crankshaft ran in a drive-side ball race and a timing-side plain bush. The wheels were cast iron, and a short integral mainshaft went on the timing side, with this length chosen to assist assembly. The drive-side mainshaft was longer and in steel, and a press fit in the flywheel where it had a serrated flange to prevent it from turning.

A single-row roller big end ran in the forged steel rod which was bushed for the gudgeon pin. The piston moved in a cast-iron barrel which was painted aluminium to match the rest of the engine and was deeply spigoted into the crankcase and up into the light alloy cylinder head. This was held on four long studs and was integral with the rocker box.

The head had the valve seats cast-in and a steel sleeve for the exhaust port. On the inlet side went a flange-mounted Amal 332 carburettor with separate float chamber and long hose to an air cleaner. The rockers oscillated on fixed spindles with adjusters at their outer ends and were enclosed by pressed steel covers, each held by a single nut.

The timing gear was of the simplest construction with the camshaft gear driven from the crankshaft, tappets above it working in the crankcase, pushrods to connect them to the rockers and a pushrod tube with seals to enclose them. The driving gear fitted into the end of the crankshaft rather than on it to keep the shaft length down and was secured by a single bolt. Incorporated with it was a skew gear. This drove a vertical shaft to the rear of the crankshaft which had two jobs to do.

The first was to drive the twin-plunger oil pump set low down in the timing chest. It did this with an offset pin at its lower end. At the top went a drive to a points cam, which went in a housing located above the crankcase and aft of the cylinder. The drive incorporated an advance mechanism and was commonly referred to as a distributor, as it was on the twins, although it was simply a points housing.

The alternator went on the left end of the crankshaft outboard of the single-strand

Road racer and special builder Geoff Monty riding a trials Cub in a 1960 Bemsee club trial more successfully than most of his fellow racers. The trials model was popular despite the troubles the energy transfer ignition system brought in its train.

Gordon Blakeway's Cub as used in the 1960 Scottish Six Days Trial, but which retired when in fourth place. Even the factory had to contend with the ignition trauma brought on by the slack drive, but did get the inboard exhaust pipe before the production models.

The T20S was built only for 1960 and was the first Cub fitted with the dreadful energy transfer ignition system. It had direct lighting with a small headlamp but heavy-duty forks from a twin and many of the details from earlier off-road models.

The T20S/L was built for enduros for 1961 and kept the energy transfer ignition. It was much as the T20S from the year before with similar off-road fittings and fixtures, but again lasted only for the one year.

primary chain which drove a three-plate clutch. This had a shock absorber built into it and attached to the mainshaft of a very English style four-speed gearbox. This ran in bushes, except for the sleeve gear which turned in a ball race, and the gears were moved by a pair of selectors. These were controlled by a quadrant-shaped cam plate which pivoted on a pin set in the right side cover.

This cover sealed off both the timing chest and the gearbox by running the full length of the crankcase. It was cast so the crankshaft could be assembled from the left, with a shallow recess on the right for the camshaft, timing gears and oil pump. The rear part was in reverse to this to provide a wall on the left, for the sleeve gear bearing and other bushes, with access for gearbox assembly from the right.

The cover on the right supported the gearchange shaft and a positive stop mechanism which moved the camplate one gear at a time. An outer cover concealed the mechanism and also the kickstart return spring, plus the clutch lever and cable end. The kickstart worked on the layshaft first gear so the engine had to be in neutral before it was started. On the other side of the engine a further cover acted as a primary-drive outer. This was spigoted to the inner as it carried the alternator stator.

The complete engine unit had a mounting lug at each end with one underneath the crankcase, and went into a loop frame with plunger rear suspension. The main-frame loop was a single tube of which both ends were flattened to join in one headstock lug. This placed heavy loads on that area of the frame but did result in a low top tube line, so the petrol tank did not need the usual tunnel formed in it.

The tank was constructed from two pressings, with the joint running along each side from front to rear mounting. These were at the headstock and seat nose, so the tank contributed to the support of the former and did have a small tunnel in its underside. This both stiffened the structure and concealed the top tube plus the wiring and controls running along it.

The front suspension was by telescopic forks which looked like those on the twins although they lacked hydraulic damping. They were of simple construction with grease lubrication, but did have the upper covers and nacelle as on the larger models. Cast-iron offset hubs with single-leading-shoe drum brakes and 19 in. steel rims were used by both wheels. The rear wheel drove the speedometer, and its brake was rod-operated while its sprocket was bolted in place. Neat, close-fitting mudguards were

Derek Adsett riding a Cub in a 1962 trial. Even then the frame was still weak and needed gussets added around the headstock. Ignition and big-end wear continued to be problems along with overheating, which the undershield aggravated. Ventilation helps.

used, with the front one unsprung to give a better line to the machine.

The oil tank for the dry-sump lubrication system went on the right beneath the saddle and was matched by a toolbox on the left. This extended across to also enclose the battery and air cleaner, so the whole was a tidy assembly. Above it went the ignition coil, but this was soon moved below the oil tank to the rear of the engine unit and its place was taken by the rectifier.

The exhaust system ran low down on the right to a short tubular silencer. The handlebars were typical Triumph but with integral pivot blocks for the clutch and brake levers and a built-in horn button. There was no air lever, as the cold-start control went on the carburettor itself, so a very neat layout resulted.

The machine style copied the larger twins with a miniature of the four-bar tank badge, while the nacelle carried the speedometer and electrics switch. There were kneegrips with the Triumph name for the petrol tank and the whole machine was finished in the famous Amaranth Red with gold lining on the mudguards. The wheel rims were chrome plated with red centres lined in gold.

The early models suffered too many problems once on the road because the Terrier was rushed into production in response to customer and trade demand. Problem areas were mainly the big ends, clutch and electrics although, except for the big end, which remained a problem area for many years, the Terrier made a nice machine that stood out among a sea of popping two-strokes. The exhaust note was altogether different and the performance adequate for the time.

The immediate changes were from Wipac to Lucas electrics, which resulted in the ignition coil move and the addition of the recti-

The T20S/H introduced in 1962 was more of a sports model than off-road so had a low exhaust system and battery ignition. It did keep the gaitered front forks and small headlamp, along with an undershield and sports mudguards. In this form it sold well and its improved engine was also used by the T20.

The TR20 trials model was amended for 1963 when the points moved into the timing cover and finned rocker lids were fitted. The machine was built solely for trials and thus had the exhaust tucked in well. Front wheel was 21 in. and no lights.

fier. The clutch was improved and a plain big end appeared, although not for the Terrier until mid 1954. Before then, a new and larger model was introduced as the Tiger Cub or T20 which had both bore and stroke increased to give a 199 cc capacity, but otherwise the engine unit was as for the Terrier.

Both models had a gear indicator added in the form of a small dial on the nacelle. The pointer was turned by a rack-and-pinion mechanism and the rack was connected by cable to a thin rod attached to the camplate. It worked quite well.

The Cub was fitted as standard with a dual seat and pillion rests which became an option for the Terrier. It also had an upswept exhaust system, so its silencer was carried at a higher level than that of the T15, although that part could be fitted as an option. The Cub finish also differed, with shell blue sheen for the tank and mudguards and black for the rest of the painted parts.

The two models ran on for 1955 with detail changes in the main, although the Cub was fitted with the low-level exhaust system and the upswept one became an option for the two machines. It was much the same with the engine units for 1956, although there was a new oil pump and the Cub changed to a new big end and a ½ in. pitch primary chain in place of the ⅜ in. one used up to then.

On the cycle side there was a larger oil tank for both machines and a new petrol tank for the Cub. This model also had the ignition coil moved back under the seat where it was enclosed by a plastic sheet, and other detail changes, the most noticeable to the wheels. In place of the original 19 in. rims with the 3.00 in. section tyres, there were 16 in. rims and 3.25 in. tyres.

The big-end change was the first of several but the plain bearing was never the best type for a single, and all proved to be the Achilles heel of the engine. Given correct lubrication there was no problem, but this meant careful warming up as well as the right grade of oil. All too often the owner was a novice or commuter, with no real mechanical knowledge, or young and enthusiastic and thus unlikely to do more than start up, leap aboard and open the throttle wide.

Under this treatment it was quite possible to ruin a big end in 100 miles or less, and dealers soon tired of warranty replacements and endeavoring to persuade customers to ride more sedately for the first few miles. Few remembered until they themselves had to pay. Most blamed the Cub, the dealer and Triumph, but never themselves.

At the end of 1956 the Terrier was dropped but the Cub was to run on for another decade or more in a variety of forms. It was to become the basis of the BSA C15 in 1958, and thus led to a whole range of models for that company which in time resulted in more Triumph singles.

For 1957 the Cub had a new frame with pivoted fork rear suspension and hydraulic damping for the front forks. It was built in two forms, with one the T20 Cub, much as before, and the other the T20C in competition form. Both models had the new frame and associated detail alterations. Among these was a new seat, a rear brake torque stay and Girling units to control the rear fork. The engine had some fins added to the rocker box and big-end modifications, while the petrol tank on the T20 was fitted with the grill badge as used by the twins that year.

The T20C was supplied with lights and the normal nacelle but its front forks did have gaiters to keep out the dirt. Its mudguards were simple blades, the tyres were 19 in. front and 18 in. rear diameter with competition treads and the upswept exhaust pipe was used with the raised silencer. The petrol tank retained the four-bar badge, a crankcase shield was fitted but had no centre stand and the gearing was lowered.

Both models had a new finish in silver-grey and continued as such for 1958 when there were few external changes. Inside there was a duplex primary chain, while on the outside went a new silencer and a deeper front mudguard for the T20. During the year both models changed over to a Zenith carburettor in place of the original Amal.

The engine finning was increased for 1959, and this was the only change easily seen on the T20C; the other changes were

This example is a 1964 T20 Cub which has timing cover points, finned rocker covers and a rod gear indicator protruding from the crankcase. It has a two-tone finish for the tank, and this continues with the contrasting toolbox lid and skirt, with the oil tank to match on the other side.

This 1965 trials TR20 Cub is little changed from the earlier version of the model. It had only one more year in production and this final form was much improved. Trials Cubs of all types served the novice rider well for over a decade and many are still running in pre-1965 trials.

internal. The T20 received these internal changes as well, but on that model it was the external changes that were more noticeable, with a skirt added to enclose the area beneath the seat but not the rear wheel. The two skirt halves had openings cut in their sides through which the oil tank and toolbox protruded, although they had to be moved to suit. The petrol tank was made deeper.

At the end of the year the T20C was replaced by the T20S which was aimed more for off-road use, with fewer concessions to the road. To this end it lost its battery and went over to energy transfer ignition which was sensitive to the points gap and the ignition timing. The lighting was direct with a small headlamp hung from the fork shrouds, and there was no nacelle so the speedometer was mounted on top of the forks.

These were heavy-duty and came from the 350 cc twin with changes to suit the frame and the addition of fork gaiters. The wheel sizes were as for the T20C and the undershield remained in place. Unlike the earlier machines, the front mudguard front stay attached to the fork leg halfway down it instead of at the bottom and this gave the parts a different line and style. The T20 also had its changes for 1960 and while most were internal, there was one easily noted, which was to 17 in. wheel rims.

During the year, from engine number 57617, both models had a major change to the engine castings without alterations to the internals. The split line between the main castings was moved over to the cylinder centre line, but the right case continued to include the complete gearbox. The inner and outer right side covers were new parts, although much as before, and the same applied to the left outer or primary chaincase cover. The left or primary inner case became the left crankcase and included the primary inner, so the number of castings stayed the same.

The T20S was replaced by two models for 1961, these being the T20T for trials and the T20S/L for enduros. Both retained the small headlamp and energy transfer ignition and had a new oil pump which was also fitted to the T20. The sporting models had wide- or close-ratio gearboxes to suit their purpose and both retained the undershield. Either could be fitted with a rev counter and if this was done a special outer timing cover was needed to accommodate the drive, plus round instruments in place of the single D-shaped speedometer. Both continued with the waist-level silencer, and the T20S/L was fitted with an Amal Monobloc carburettor of the same type used on the T20S. Both models were dropped before the end of the year.

The enduro model became the T20S/S for 1962 and while it continued for export for several years, it was soon replaced on the home market by the T20S/H. The first of these was little changed from the T20S/L but did have a low-level exhaust system, although the raised one remained an option with a further-raised pipe to be used when the rev counter was fitted. Otherwise, the T20S/S remained with the energy transfer

ignition, direct lights and old-style tank badge.

The T20S/H differed far more than a superficial glance showed. The overall lines stayed much as before but the accent moved away from the off-road or trail use to the sports roadster. To this end the energy transfer ignition was replaced by a battery and coil system. The toolbox and battery housing was similar to the T20's with an air filter built in, but the fork gaiters and blade mudguards remained. The electric switches moved to brackets beneath the seat, so there was only the dipswitch left in the headlamp shell, and the petrol tank carried the grill-type badges.

Inside the engine there was a change to the crankshaft, so the timing-side mainshaft became a pressed-in part supported by a ball race main bearing. In addition, the timing spur gear and the oil pump plus contact breaker skew gear became separate parts and a two-part crankpin was fitted. The lubrication system was modified to suit the

The T20 became the Bantam Cub for 1966 and lost its skirt. It used the frame from the BSA model along with the forks of which the legs were common anyway as were the hubs. The oil tank and toolbox lines were copied from the BSA as were many details, but the tank stayed Triumph.

revised timing side and the oil pump capacity increased.

This engine went into the T20 early in the year, but otherwise that model had few changes other than to a two-tone finish in flame and silver-grey. A gradual change occurred with export models, fitting an Amal 32, while the home market stayed with the Zenith for much of the year although in the end the Amal was used for all.

The range was expanded early in 1962, when the T20S/H appeared, with two more models, both of which used its engine with minor alterations. These were the TR20 for trials and TS20 for scrambles. The first had a low compression ratio and wide gears while the second had high compression and close gears. Both had energy transfer ignition, a short seat, and the right side tube of the rear subframe was modified to allow the exhaust to run inboard of it. The pipes ran at waist level and a small tubular silencer went on the trials machine, whereas the scrambler simply had an open pipe. Both models had alloy

mudguards and the heavy-duty front fork with gaiters, and both had the footrests strengthened while those on the TR20 were moved a little to the rear.

All four models continued for 1963 with one obvious change: the contact breaker was moved into the timing cover where its cam was driven from the camshaft. This was a great help to the energy transfer ignition, but it still had its own set of advance springs and points cam to keep it on top line.

A further useful change to the timing cover was a hole aft of the kickstart shaft. This hole gave access to the end of the clutch lever so the cable could be changed without removing the cover, and a rubber bung normally sealed it. One other external change to the engine was that the rocker covers were finned, although their single-nut fixing remained as before.

The competition models had no other changes but the road models lost the gear indicator on the nacelle. This was replaced by a plunger that rose out of the crankcase

The final form of the Triumph single was the T20S/C Super Cub built first in 1967. It used the parts from the Bantam Cub of the year before, with a Bantam tank in place of the Triumph one, an old-style tank badge and full-width hubs for both wheels.

and was directly linked to the camplate. The T20 changed to twin switches in the nacelle to control its electrics, and the paint on the oil tank and toolbox lid was altered so it matched the petrol tank top and contrasted with the skirt colour.

There was little visible change for any model for 1964 other than to a hi-fi scarlet finish to go with the silver-grey and black, while the T20S/H lost its undershield. At the end of the season the TS20 was dropped from the list but the numbers were made up

Although Triumph stopped building the Cub in any form in 1968, riders continued to use the engine unit for other machines. This one is a 1969 Cheetah being ridden in the Scottish Six Days that year. There were other firms that made similar models.

for 1965 with the T20SM. This was a trail model, sold in the United States as the Mountain Cub, and painted yellow to avoid shooting accidents out in the wilds. There were few changes for the other models, but the gear indicator was deleted once and for all and a longer, cranked kickstart went on the T20S/H. It and the TR20 also had new fork sliders.

The road T20 Tiger Cub had a major revamp to its cycle parts for 1966, when it was given the BSA Bantam frame and became known as the Bantam Cub. It lost the rear enclosure and nacelle, while the forks and hubs had been common to both models for some time. The headlamp was from a Bantam, was long enough to carry the speedometer and was chrome plated while the oil tank was shaped to match the Bantam-style centre and left side panels. These continued to house the battery and tool kit but not the pancake air filter, which was attached directly to the carburettor. The petrol tank remained the usual Cub type with grill badge, but the mudguards were Bantam and 18 in. wheels were used.

Inside the engine went a revised oil pump drive and at last, the much needed roller big end. Externally, the engine appearance was altered with head and barrel castings of a more square cross-section, but neither changed its material.

Only the basic model continued for 1967 when it was renamed the Super Cub. The changes were fairly minimal but did include full-width hubs for the brakes, which remained the same 5½ in. they had always been. The front mudguard stays became more sporting and the front stay and bridge attached much higher on the fork legs than before. The seat and petrol tank changed with a reversion to the four-bar styling for the latter which was a Bantam part with only the name changed.

The model ran on into 1968 without change but was dropped during the year, bringing the Cub line to an end. After this the firm concentrated on its twins and triples, although the singles did make a further appearance even if only as BSAs with a change of clothes.

Prospects

These models never rate more than three stars simply because small is less popular than large. The older trials models do better than one might expect, for they can be used in pre-1965 trials events.

For general reliability the later machines are the best choice, since eventually the fragile big end and inadequate oil pump were improved. Both went through a good many changes over the years and are the weak points of the design. The energy transfer ignition system was always a problem and is best avoided, but the use of modern electrics can cure this without departing noticeably from the external looks.

Terriers are rare machines now, so rate three stars on that count, as do the early Cubs in the plunger frame. They then drop to two stars when in the pivoted fork frame, with or without a skirt, but then down to one once the points moved into the timing chest in 1963. Not that these were bad Cubs, they were in fact better than their predecessors for riding, but less so as an investment. The last models—the Bantam and Super Cubs—have the advantage that many BSA parts can be used, thus easing any spares sourcing problems. So both Terrier and Cub are again for riding rather than saving.

The off-road Cubs began with the T20C which was followed by the T20T, both of which get three stars for pre-1965 trial use. The T20S and T20S/L rate two stars as do the T20S/S and T20S/H, except for the 1962 versions which get three for having the points housing and thus being less common. The energy transfer ignition remains a major snag until dealt with.

The TR20 rates three stars for 1962 for the same reason, with two for 1963-64 but only one for 1965-66, as it becomes too young for pre-1965 trials use. The TS20 follows the same pattern, for it can readily be modified for these events but only ran to 1964. Finally, the T20SM rates two stars for being a low-volume model and rare in its own country.

Trophy, Blazer and Avenger

These three models were BSA clones thus were all produced at Small Heath, but all had their origins in the original Triumph Terrier although much developed from those early days. The process took some years to happen, but in time that small 149 cc engine grew to a full 499 cc and in the process sparked off a whole range of models.

The first expansion was to create the 199 cc Cub, but in 1958 this was taken further and the outcome was the 247 cc BSA C15. This differed from the Triumph in having a vertical cylinder and central crankcase joint line, but most of the other features were there. The points housing had to lay back at an angle to clear the cylinder, so the oil pump lay forward to stay in line with it, and at the top there was a separate rocker box.

The internal construction was as for the Cub, other than the oil pump which was the usual BSA gear type, and the primary drive, four-speed gearbox and gear selection mechanism duplicated the Triumph. The plain big end, timing-side bush and drive-side ball race main were all the same, as was the simple gear drive to the camshaft with its tappet followers and pushrods housed within a tube up to the cylinder head.

The C15 had a conventional set of cycle parts with loop frame, telescopic front and pivoted rear forks, full-width hubs and drum brakes. It was popular and soon was joined by a pair of competition versions—a sports model and the 343 cc B40 which was also built in sports form.

For 1967 the C15 became the C25 Barracuda and the engine had a number of significant changes. Internally there was a one-piece crankshaft with two flywheel rings bolted to it and an alloy rod with split big end. Ball and roller race mains were fitted to the crankcase which remained much as before.

The head and barrel were both light alloy, with a sleeve for the cylinder, and their fins were cast to a close pitch and square shape. This enclosed the pushrods within the barrel and gave a distinctive line to the engine. The top half was otherwise as before, as was the timing side except that the contact points were now mounted in the cover and their cam driven from the camshaft. The oil pump mounting was altered but it remained a skew-driven gear pump.

The TR25W was introduced in 1968 in this form with inboard exhaust pipe. It was a clone of two BSAs, and used the B25 engine and the off-road cycle parts from a larger single. The badges, finish and a couple of covers were altered to indicate a Triumph, but it was not a success.

The primary drive included a tensioner for the duplex chain and the alternator went on the left end of the crankshaft. The clutch, with its transmission shock absorber, was typical of Triumph or BSA, and the gearbox and its change mechanism was much as the original Terrier. The main alteration was to the kickstart which became a quadrant meshing with a mainshaft-mounted ratchet gear. The clutch lift also changed to a rack-and-pinion design, with an external lever on the end of the gear shaft.

This then was the engine used by the Triumph Trophy TR25W introduced in 1968 for trail use as well as on the road. It differed from the BSA Starfire in not having a valve-lifter mechanism in the rocker box and the Triumph logo on the side cover. Otherwise it was the same unit with just one tooth less on the gearbox sprocket to lower the gearing.

The basic cycle parts were the same, so the frame, forks and wheels were common. However, the two makes looked quite different, for the rest of the parts were to suit the machine purpose or styled for the

marque. As a start, the Triumph exhaust system ran at waist level on the right with the pipe tucked inside the frame under the oil tank, with a small tubular silencer plus heat shield at its end.

The petrol tank carried the eyebrow tank badges while the dual seat was ribbed and without a tail hump. The footrests folded, and there was no centre stand but there was a prop and an undershield. Large, triangular side covers enclosed the oil tank and battery and carried the name Trophy 250 on each side, and the headlamp was small with the switches mounted on it.

The wheels were 19 in. front and 18 in. rear and had trail tyres but, while the front had a full-width hub, the rear was the old BSA crinkle hub with separate brake drum and bolted-on sprocket. Single-leading-shoe drum brakes were used as well as sports mudguards, the rear one being supported by a stay that incorporated a seat rail. It was also the mounting for the rear side reflectors; the front ones went under the nose of the fuel tank with the horn.

The Trophy was given the twin-leading-shoe front brake with bell-crank lever for 1969, along with a new exhaust pipe that ran outside the frame. This was to cater to a larger silencer with wire mesh heat shield, and the tank badge changed to the picture-frame type. The exhaust changed again for 1970 when it was moved over to the left, and for that year an oil-pressure switch was added and a warning light appeared in the headlamp shell. This was the last season for the Trophy which was replaced by two new models for 1971.

These were nearly identical and were listed as the T25SS Blazer SS Street Scrambler and T25T Trail Blazer Trail Bike, both with the same 247 cc engine as before. The one was completely new, and common to the BSA marque as well, with the engine oil carried within its large-diameter downtube. This was matched by a top tube of larger size with the two linked by duplex ones under

the engine and up to the seat nose. A further welded-on subframe supported the seat and rear fork units.

The oil was taken from the base of the downtube, which had a filter in it, to the engine and returned via an external filter to the headstock area. The frame was thus not unlike the works motocross frame and had needle roller bearings for the rear fork, whose pivot point was moved by a camplate to set the rear chain tension.

The front forks were the group slimline type with four-stud fixing for the wheel spindle caps, internal springs and no gaiters. The wheels, front and rear, had conical hubs and the back one contained a single-leading shoe brake and was supported in an 18 in. rim. A similar brake and a 20 in. rim went on the front wheel of the T25T, but the T25SS had the twin-leading shoe brake with short cam levers that were pulled together by

For 1970 the TR25W moved its exhaust system over to the left but was otherwise still a BSA in all but name. The engine has a poor reputation for oil leaks, wear and weak internals, which is deserved. It can be improved if carefully put together by an expert.

cable. It also had an 18 in. rim and both models had tyres to suit their purpose.

Most of the other parts were common to both models and these included the exhaust system. The pipe for this curled along the right side of the engine to pass inside the frame tube where it joined a lozenge-shaped silencer. This ran up at an angle to terminate with a high-level tailpipe and both this and the main body had perforated heat shields attached to them.

The mudguards did differ with the road model, having the front one held close to the wheel by wire stays which were rubber-mounted to the lower fork legs. On the trail bike the guard was attached to the bottom fork crown, so sat well clear of the tyre.

The side panels were smaller than before and carried different legends, while the tank finish was new, with graphics and a name transfer. The electrics went in a box under its nose with reflectors attached to each side

TRIUMPH BLAZER SS 250

New versions of the singles were launched for 1971 and this is the Triumph Blazer T25SS. Like the trail version listed as the T25T, it had an oil-carrying frame, conical hubs and was a copy of the equivalent BSA with many group fitments. The engines continued to be frail and all the models had a short production life.

and both models came fitted with turn signals.

The models had a short life, for the BSA group was in serious financial trouble and the problems at Small Heath soon brought production to an end. This really ought to have been the end of the singles but there was one more BSA clone to come.

This was the TR5MX Avenger which was built in small numbers in 1973 for motocross use. It was a BSA B50MX with minor changes and this was the final stretch of the old Terrier. From the C15 had come the 343 cc B40 and later the 441 cc B44, but for 1971 BSA had opened up the engine to the full 499 cc to create the B50.

Inside it went a built-up crankshaft with caged roller big end, and this had an extra ball race on the drive side to support it. Otherwise it was much as the 247 cc unit, although there were detail differences. The chassis side was from the T25T but amended for motocross, with competition plates and air filter. The wheels kept their conical hubs, but the front carried a 21 in. rim while the handlebars were braced and the fuel tank small and in alloy.

The exhaust system was the oddest feature. While the pipe was as on the 250, it connected to a junction to which two silencers were fastened. These were of the reverse cone megaphone form and mounted one above the other to deal with the big bangs from the engine, which they managed well.

It was the end of the line for the type of machine that could ride the trails in its own special way. Modern engines lack the easy manner of the older ones which thumped along, mostly without changing gear. And the nice ride without stress seems to have gone forever.

Prospects

I've given two stars apiece for this lot, which fall between too many stools to be popular. To a Triumph fanatic they are not real examples of the marque, and for the rest of us—well, we might as well find a BSA.

The Avenger is too late for pre-1965 events and thus fails to fit in well anywhere, but the others make an acceptable choice against the BSA if that is what you seek. Watch out for hybrids and mongrels!

US Variants

These began as early as 1958 with the T20J and T20CA. The first was a Junior model, restricted to 5 bhp by a carburettor modification and offered into 1961. The second was a US version of the T20C with a low-level exhaust system and road tyres, available for only two seasons.

Next came the T20W, a road version of the T20T fitted with lights; few were sold in its single 1960 model year. It was 1962 before the next machines appeared, the T20SC and T20SR. The first was in off-road form with high-compression piston, sports cam, trials tyres and upswept exhaust system. It was fitted with a Monobloc carburettor and retained the standard gearbox. The second was based on the T20SC but had road tyres, low-level exhaust and close-ratio gears. Both models were listed to 1965.

For 1964 there was the T20SM, similar to the T20SC but with wide-ratio gears, low-compression piston, energy-transfer ignition and lights. It ran on to 1968 but in 1966 was joined by the T20M, a similar model that continued on to 1970.

Prospects

In line with the stock range, maybe a star or half more as fewer were built and they all went to the same country. A few may have returned home, but not many.

Chapter 7

War and racing

★★★★★	3TW twin 1940
★★★★★	5TW twin 1942
★★★★★	TRW prototype 1946
★★	3SW 343 cc 1940-45
★★	5SW 493 cc 1940-45
★★	3HW 343 cc 1940-45
★★★	Generator 1940-45
★★	TRW twin 1950-65
★★★★★	GP Grand Prix 1948-50
★★★★	T100 Tiger 100 plus kit 1951-53
★★★★	T100c Tiger 100 1953

War might be considered the ultimate competition and, while this book concerns postwar models, the wartime machines and what evolved from them did impinge on that later era. Racing of any kind has always been a form of solo or team war, so the two aspects tie together.

The wartime machines were mainly singles based on prewar models, but there was

The bulk of Triumph's wartime production was of the 343 cc ohv single model 3HW which was based on the prewar machines. It used most of their parts but did gain a one-piece head and rocker box. A tough engine that was much used in postwar competitions.

work done on twins and from this came a postwar service model. This was built over a span of fifteen years but without any major change, so that the service stores had no real problems with spare parts while the machines all retained their Triumph line.

Racing was generally taboo at Triumph while Edward Turner was in charge. Before the war the only concessions to it were the 493 cc ohv 5/10 singles of 1934-36, and for the twins the bronze head and megaphone silencers of the Tiger 100. This situation had been strengthened by a disaster at the 1934 TT when a team of singles all retired, but in spite of that a Triumph held the all-time 350 and 750 cc Brooklands lap records.

Turner always insisted that racing did not pay, but when he was away members of the firm would indulge their urge to build faster engines. He did concur with one exercise in 1946, and from this came the major postwar racing Triumph model, the Grand Prix, which, while never a total success, did offer an alternative to the Manx Norton of the time until the Norton gained its featherbed frame.

Military machines

During the war the bulk of Triumph production was of the 343 cc single-cylinder 3HW model with overhead valves, together with some 3SW and 5SW machines with 343 and 493 cc side-valve engines. All were much as their prewar equivalents and thus had many common parts.

About the only real change was to the ohv model which had the rocker box cast integral with the head and simple covers to give access to the valve adjusters and pushrod ends. Otherwise they were simple adaptations. The differences between the three machines used by the services were minimal, and it was the 3HW that was proposed to be demobbed in 1945 to join the civilian model range.

These ex-service machines have their own group of enthusiasts, so are collected as much as many others. Finding a complete 3HW is now no easy task; most that survive have been altered in some way. In the early postwar years the Triumph, along with others, was sold off by the war office in batches to dealers who gave them a quick respray in black or maroon. They were soon snapped up by a transport-hungry public and served them well until postwar production could satisfy their needs.

Quite a number of these machines finished up in competition. The engine was tough and ran well on alcohol fuel while the rest of the parts could be adapted for the

This ohv twin-cylinder 3TW was built as a prototype during the war but was never destined to go into production. Its internal engine construction differed from the prewar twins, and other unusual features were the gearbox which bolted to the back of the crankcase and the petrol tank which was a stressed frame member.

The one-off 5TW, built to make a point but an indication of the road ahead. It had a side-valve engine with internals from the Speed Twin but the camshaft was chain driven. It was the first Triumph to have telescopic front forks and thus looks much like the early postwar machines.

This TRW model was built in 1956 as part of an order for Pakistan and thus used the cycle parts of that era with the rigid frame. This was typical of the build standard. Machines also went to Canada and the Paris police, with coil ignition being used from 1956.

grass-track or scrambles events of the times, and a few even went road racing. Spares were easy and cheap to buy so the model

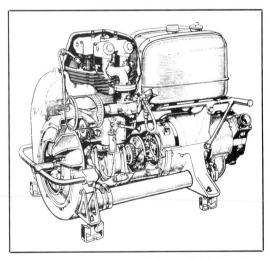

The wartime generator unit from which the alloy head of the postwar TR5 and GP models came. The internals differ a good deal from the road engines, as the inlet and exhaust are transposed, but this unlikely product led to some nice machines after the war.

provided a solution to the shortage of *real* racers.

The other military models were twins, and the first was designed early in the war to meet a Ministry specification for a single machine to be built by all firms. Edward Turner cut through the development time by using the Tiger 85 as the basis, with its one-piece head and rocker box, and clamped-up crankshaft. The result was the 3TW.

In its original form the engine had a light alloy head and barrel to keep the weight down and an alternator for the direct lighting set in the timing chest. Later, the top half became iron when alloy was in short supply and the generator was moved into the primary chaincase, where it was driven from the left end of the crankshaft. Magneto ignition was retained and the exhaust system had a two-into-one pipe feeding a waist-level silencer on the left, rather similar to the postwar TR5.

There were only three speeds in the gearbox which was bolted to the rear of the crankcase and driven by a duplex chain with a slipper tensioner. The whole unit went into a rigid cradle frame with girder forks, and the frame was conventional except for the top tube. This was formed from a channel section which bolted between the headstock and seat nose to form a structural member. Deep pressings were seam welded to this on each side to produce the petrol tank. This construction made the tank easy to make and increased its capacity.

The remainder of the machine conformed with normal practice, with drum brakes, 19 in. wheels, saddle, oil tank beneath it on the right and small rear carrier. An air cleaner went beside the oil tank, there was a small headlight and only a bulb horn.

The special aspect of the machine was its light weight. In original form, where even the footrests were light alloy, it scaled a mere 230 lb. With an engine that came on above 3000 rpm it was a flyer and too fast for the War Office, but more flywheel weight and less carburettor sorted that out. With the iron engine its weight rose to just over 260 lb., but in this form it was still very easy to ride on track or road as required in service use.

Sadly for Triumph, the Coventry factory was bombed out of existence late in 1940 and all plans for the 3TW were shelved. The firm finally moved to Meriden, but before then simply got on with the task of building singles as fast as they could and continued with this to the end of the war.

Twins were not forgotten, though, and in late 1942 the 5TW was built mainly to make a political point against BSA where Turner was briefly working. It had a side-valve engine of 499 cc with much of the bottom half internals taken from the Speed Twin. A single camshaft ran across the front of the engine, with the four valves above it, and was chain-driven from the crankshaft. The chain also drove the dynamo, which occupied the normal magneto position, and this incorporated the contact points and automatic advance for the coil ignition. The chain was slipper tensioned and the camshaft drove a twin-plunger oil pump.

The cylinders were cast as one block with the carburettor at the back, so there was a tricky passage through this to the valves. The exhausts simply fed into a pipe and silencer on each side and were mainly stock

The alloy top half of the Triumph Grand Prix road-racing machine showing the cowling bosses on the block casting. Twin Amals were crammed in on the parallel ports with a single remote float chamber, which hung beside the oil tank.

parts, as was most of the rest of the machine. The one new point was the use of telescopic front forks with hydraulic damping, which tidied up the front end. Other items such as tank, saddle, four-speed gearbox and the wheels were all as used by the singles.

The 5TW was shown to the outside world early in 1943 on a wet day when short test

Don Crossley with the Grand Prix, on which he won the 1948 Manx Senior by over three minutes. This must have been some compensation to the firm for the many retirements they suffered in the TT that year.

A restored Grand Prix on show—and very nice too. Handling was not up to the standards of the old Garden Gate Norton plunger frame, so well below the featherbed when that appeared and set the norm. The sprung hub was hardly an asset, so private owners often built their own frames with pivoted fork rear suspension.

rides showed up its flexibility and ease of use in poor conditions. After that it was packed away and it was 1946 before anything fresh occurred. By then the war was over and the demand for military machines had gone—the services had more than they knew what to do with.

Another Ministry specification had been drawn up, however, and to meet this Triumph produced the TRW which was a mixture of 3TW and 5TW designs in the engine department. The crankshaft used the clamped design from the 3TW, but the camshaft was gear driven via a large idler that also drove a rear-mounted magneto. The oil pump was, as usual, driven from the end of the camshaft, and an alternator went on the left end of the crankshaft.

Both head and block were in light alloy on the early examples to keep the weight down, and the carburettor still went at the rear. The exhausts were splayed from the corners of the block and ran to an expansion box in front of the crankcase, with a single pipe and silencer low down on the right.

The transmission was by a three-speed gearbox at first, with this driven by a duplex chain with a slipper tensioner, although the box was separate from the engine. The frame was much as the 3TW with the fuel tank acting as a brace, but telescopic front forks were fitted.

The machine answered the specification but by then there was no real call for more service motorcycles, so it began to undergo peacetime Ministry development. After undergoing their special, drawn-out procedures, in time the machine became the Hybrid to Triumph staff although it kept the TRW model name.

The Hybrid took the TRW engine and fitted it into the most suitable frame and cycle parts that came from the assembly line. In 1950, when the first production batch was made, this meant the TR5 as this kept the weight down and brought in the off-road items necessary to a service machine. It thus had the special trials frame, normal four-speed gearbox, nacelle and Trophy wheels along with the military equipment the services required.

From then on the TRW stayed stuck as if in a time warp. The engine remained as it was, but with an iron block, and continued with its complex but economical Solex carburettor. The only obvious change was to coil ignition in 1956. The points housing went in the old magneto position and the coils up under the tank. The cycle side plus the gearbox stuck to its 1950 form, to suit service procurement no doubt, with few alterations.

One machine was built in a pivoted fork frame, but the services stuck to the original rigid one for the rest. By the time the last TRW was built in 1965, there were nearly 6,000 of them. By then the limited power was beginning to become a handicap on main roads and the lack of rear suspension no help on the rough.

The services began to change over to other machines, and these were based much more on the standard Cub or unit construction Tiger 100 models, with minimal modifications. Aside from colour, many of the changes were commonly made for police or other public utility machines, and all this helped to keep the costs down.

The Triumph company was involved with a number of projects outside the motorcycle field during the war, and the best known of these was a portable generator for the RAF. This had to be light enough to be carried by two men, and although the engine used in it seemed to be a Speed Twin it was changed a good deal. Few parts remained exactly as for the motorcycle, and the ones that mattered for the future were the head and barrel.

These were both cast in light alloy, with inserts to suit the valves and fittings, and in a rectangular form with regular finning. This enabled cowling to be attached round the top half, and a crankshaft-mounted fan forced cooling air over the fins. To suit the installation the exhaust ports were parallel, and it was this head and barrel that went on the early TR5 models of 1949-50.

The whole unit was different from the usual low-output stationary engines used by the services—it would fire up easily and run as if it meant it. The others would chug slowly, and the time it took between throttle opening and engine response could seem minutes apart. The Triumph generator wound up like the motorcycle engine it was, and gave a good few NCOs an anxious moment when an erk blipped the lever. It was soon realized that it could throw a rod if

The amount of tuning data on the Triumph twin made it a popular one for road-racing specials, and the low height was an added bonus for sidecar use. This outfit has gone further, but the engine design makes the reversal easy to do as the heads and camshafts can be switched round without trouble.

For many years the T120 was the leading machine in production racing; this is a typical example. Some of the fastest were the most standard looking, and tuners found the engine responded well to known techniques and careful assembly.

abused and if you had signed for it, you made sure it stayed in one piece and ran only at slow speeds.

Prospects

These boil down to five stars for the one-offs or prototypes and two stars for the rest. The first are so rare and change hands so seldom that they must be up at the top of the scale for interest and investment. The others depend very much on completeness and whether in military garb, but are collected only by people with an enthusiasm for the services.

A nice complete TRW is a good find if you are after that sort of thing but less so if military motorcycles fail to raise your heart rate. If you do like them, it will go well with your other military memorabilia whether a uniform, other motorcycles, weapons or tracked vehicles. However, the demand is limited and not all Triumph riders and owners will be interested, so only two stars are awarded.

The generator unit could rate three if you can find one, but it can only ever be a static exhibit and motorcycling should be an active hobby.

Road-racing machinery

The postwar activity in the racing world began with the use of the light alloy top half from the generator engine when, soon after the war, Ernie Lyons persuaded Edward Turner to provide him with a quick engine for road racing. The preparation was carried out by the brilliant Freddie Clarke, the man who held the two Brooklands records mentioned earlier. He built up a Tiger 100 with the generator top half. Inside went hot cams and pistons with as high a ratio as the pool petrol of the day would allow, while most of the detail parts were worked on in some way.

The result was history. Lyons won the 1946 Manx Grand Prix, run in appalling weather, and also set the fastest time at the famous Shelsley Walsh hillclimb that autumn. Under the pressure this generated, Turner agreed to build a batch of fifty replicas, and for David Whitworth to ride a semi-works version in 1947.

The new model did not reach the public until 1948 and was called the Grand Prix. It was much like the Lyons machine so was based firmly on the standard Tiger 100. The light alloy top half was used with suitable adjustments for racing use, so there were twin Amal carburettors with the float chamber remotely mounted next to the oil tank. This was larger than usual, as was the petrol tank which was the standard Tiger one, but with the knee recesses omitted.

The cycle parts were basically stock with minimal change, as most of what was needed came from leaving off parts. The sprung hub was fitted, which must have enlivened the ride, and an 8 in. front brake helped to stop the model. Alloy rims and mudguards were as normal for any racing machine, as were the steering damper and megaphone exhausts.

Turner's forebodings came true at the 1948 TT when all seven Triumphs that started fell by the wayside. By way of consolation Don Crossley won the Manx and Whitworth had some success in Europe, while private owners found the GP faster than the Manx Norton even if the handling was not as good. This situation lasted only until the Norton appeared with the featherbed frame, and from then on the GP was reduced to club events and making up the numbers.

Between 150 and 200 Grand Prix machines were made from 1948 to 1950 and they were exported all over the world. At

For a brief period Triumph offered the production-racing Thruxton Bonneville with all the right goodies. The option list was always a bone of contention, as some items turned out to be more available to some riders than others. But most people preferred it to this model where the factory did the selecting for you.

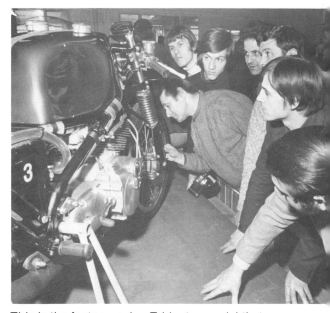

This is the factory racing Trident, a model that was successful for a time at home and abroad. There were wins in five Production Tourist Trophys in a row and on many English short circuits. The howl of the exhaust note is remembered by all who heard it at the time.

that time they were competitive but fragile, and inclined to go bang if revved too hard due, in part, to the long engine stroke. Before long, technology caught up and Triumph, as a firm, preferred to concentrate on their road models so the Grand Prix had a short model life. Private owners kept some running but often in another frame and set of cycle parts, so few now remain in original form.

Triumph did not abandon the speed market completely after 1950, as they introduced a racing kit for the Tiger 100 in 1951. This was supplied as a boxed set of parts, any of which could be bought as spares. Thus an owner could make up the simpler cycle parts and only buy the speed items needed.

For the engine there were high-compression pistons with a choice of ratios, new camshafts, stronger valve springs, a gasket set and the detail parts to convert to twin carburettors. These remained standard Amals but with a remote float chamber hung from a bracket alongside the oil tank. This had a quick-action filler cap and was larger than standard, so use with the float chamber meant removal of the battery.

All the electrics were left off in competition, so the nacelle simply carried the front racing plate and the rev counter whose drive box replaced the dynamo. On the exhaust side there were new pipes with megaphones or extensions, and the footrest kit moved the rider's feet back along with the rear brake pedal and allowed the right rest to fold up. This was to accommodate the folding kickstart pedal which replaced the stock item. A new handlebar bend was supplied,

Rather special Trident and TR6R owned by Eric Parr. The triple has a Rob North frame and many race-style parts to make a fast road motorcycle with a beautiful finish. Suffice to say, it won the top award at the 1984 Classic Bike show in England.

but not close-ratio gears, although these were available along with a range of sprockets to alter the gearing.

There were also front and rear racing mudguards available, although not in the kit, with the front from the TR5. Finally, for events that allowed the use of alcohol fuel, there was an iron cylinder block, 12:1 pistons, and parts to allow the fuel flow to the carburettors to increase.

The racing kit was available up to 1953 and for that year alone it was joined by the T100c model. This was a Tiger 100 fitted with much from the racing kit in the engine, so it had the hotter camshafts and twin carburettors. It retained the road equipment including the lights, dynamo and battery, so the float chamber had to be moved and went to a position in front of the oil tank. This remained the larger size but with a bracket on its front face for the chamber. The road silencers were fitted along with the normal footrests, but the folding kickstart was specified.

The model was listed only for the one year, after which both it and the race kit were dropped. Neither proved too popular, for the Tiger 100 was seen as a club or entry-level racer only and riders in that class normally bought a secondhand machine and just the race parts they felt they needed and could afford. Few could manage the T100c as new and few wished for all the oddments of the race kit which they could make or find more easily and at less cost.

In later years Triumph went down the option path and offered the splayed-head and twin-carburettor kits for both sizes of twin, while the firm kept to building standard machines with a list of optional parts the owner could fit.

Prospects

A definite five stars are awarded for a complete Grand Prix.

The T100c is definitely a four-star, maybe even a five, for it is a rare model built only for the one year. If one is offered, do check it over carefully to make sure it is totally genuine. A Tiger 100 with the race kit rates the same four stars and the same warning for identical reasons.

All the accumulated knowledge of tuning Triumph engines, plus modern materials, plus use of later engine internals, plus alcohol fuel made the vintage twin a potent machine. This is from the late 1970s and the girder forks made for exciting handling.

Be careful of any machine claimed to have been used by a well-known rider or in a particular event. That T110 might be the one used by Mike Hailwood and Dan Shorey to win the Thruxton 500 in 1958, but it is more likely that Stan Hailwood had it back in the King's showrooms the next day marked up "one owner—low mileage."

The same applies to early Grand Prix and late Trident machines in racing trim. They may have an authentic history but it must be fully checked out.

Cubs

The Cub was offered in military form in the 1960s, first as the T20WD based on the T20T with lights, speedometer, dualseat and centre stand. It was available from 1963 to 1965 and replaced in 1967 by the T20MWD. This was much the same, having wide-ratio gears, and was offered up to 1969.

Prospects

Rare, so good.

Chapter 8

Prototypes and works specials

Often Triumph's prototype machines were destroyed or dismantled so some of their parts could be used for other work, but some still exist, either in museums or private hands. The military models have already been mentioned, but there were also civilian models which are covered in this chapter.

In addition to the prototypes, which are generally well documented and unique in their own special ways, there are also the

The Quadrant, which looks much like a stock T160 and was based on the triple. It was built in 1974 and after some initial runs was put to one side, after which it went to the National Motorcycle Museum near Birmingham where it was renovated before going on display.

works special machines used in trials, scrambles and road racing. These generally fell between standard models and out-and-out specials; factory policy was that the works machines should look standard on the outside even if modified internally.

Most were indeed modified, and there were often other discreet alterations to improve performance in its fullest sense, reliability or speed of servicing. In fact, this last point reached its zenith on machines prepared for the ISDT, where punctures had to be mended in under five minutes, so the wheels had to come out and go back in quickly.

Be extremely careful when offered a machine that is claimed to be ex-factory and to have been used by a works rider or in a particular event. Genuine models are few and far between but the other sort are far more common. Some will be offered by an owner who honestly believes that the machine is what he claims it to be. Others will not.

The following sections cover the prototypes known to have survived, but not the competition models.

Quadrant

This four-cylinder machine was the natural development of the Trident triple and was built in 1974. So neatly was the work done that it is easy to mistake it for a stock T160 until closer inspection reveals a little more width, and that each middle exhaust pipe has its own port to attach to.

The engine was built up using parts from the triple, altered as required. The crankcase was easily assembled, with an extra centre section added to the existing one and the normal outers kept as usual. The crankshaft was less so, as it had to be built up from sections pressed together. The experimental department was never happy that it would stay in line if driven really hard. For the top half, they took two triple blocks and heads and machined one cylinder away from each before welding the two resultant twin sections together, to produce the four-cylinder parts.

The remainder of the engine was made in the same cut-and-shut manner or built up

The original Bandit was designed by Edward Turner with an all-alloy engine and gear-driven overhead camshafts. It differed from his other twin designs in having a 180 degree crankshaft, and was built too light for its speed. Along with the frail frame and forks went a mechanical disc front brake. This machine is at a 1988 classic bike show.

with stock parts. The result was wider than usual and although it was offset a little to the left in the frame, the timing cover over the alternator stuck out quite a bit. To clear this

The final engine of the Bandit was different, with a long chain drive up to the twin camshafts on the timing side. The location of the points on a camshaft end showed a lack of learning from Cub energy transfer troubles, and the machine never reached production.

the gearchange lever was reversed and the footrests moved back, but otherwise the transmission was stock Trident. There were four carburettors and four exhaust pipes, with each pair of the latter connecting to a single silencer, one on each side, while the cycle parts originated from a BSA Rocket 3 and had been used earlier for an exercise with an overhead camshaft for the Trident.

The complete machine was run early in 1975 and worked well enough to prove its point. It was never run with other than mild cams, because of the doubts about the crankshaft, so its performance was not developed and within months it was pushed to one side

on a management decision to concentrate on other matters.

In later years it was purchased by the National Motorcycle Museum who refurbished it to place it on show.

Triples

Thunderbird III was a T160 built toward the end of 1973 with engine and frame number T160-001. It was much like the machine that reached the public in 1975, although it had the T150V petrol tank.

Triumph intended to give the new model the Thunderbird III name, and decals for this were produced, but the makers of the TV

TRIUMPH BANDIT SS 350

Publicity photo of the SS350 Bandit with its many group parts and own stylish exhaust pipes. The model was one of many launched

late in 1970 for the next season, and was quickly cut from the line-up, although the group parts appeared on several BSA and Triumph models.

The early postwar economy 3TU prototype with three-speed engine unit and disc wheels. It was intended to revive the New Imperial name, but the prototype was so bad it was never proceeded with. Who would, with the twins selling so well?

programme *Thunderbirds* protested and the idea had to be dropped. Some of these decals are known to have reached private hands and thus there are other machines in existence carrying the Thunderbird III name. These may be found in Australia, New Zealand and the United States as well as their home country, but are normal Tridents.

While working on the T160, the factory considered more capacity as a means of uprating the performance. To obtain this, the engine was bored and stroked to something between 850 and 870 cc as the T180. The result was fitted to the normal T160 set of cycle parts and produced even more low-down performance than usual.

Only two engines were built, and the second was fitted into a Norton Commando frame with its special mountings for the engine, gearbox and rear fork unit. These were taken as one and attached to the main-frame by special rubber mountings to isolate it from vibration. For the Norton twin it was known as the Isolastic mounting, so it was

perhaps inevitable that the triple was called the Trisolastic.

The factory also built a triple engine with an overhead camshaft around 1970. The single camshaft was driven by a toothed belt on the right side of the engine from the exhaust camshaft gear. It thus took over the normal points housing which was then moved to the inlet camshaft gear. Aside from this and the belt cover the machine looked much like any other Trident.

There were also engines with the crank-shaft throws not at the usual 120 degrees, but like a four at 180 with one cylinder missing. This meant two quick bangs and then a long 360 degree pause before the next one.

Overhead camshaft twins

Triumph did try ohc on the 650 engine as an experiment, but in this area are best known for the 350 twin which became the Bandit but never reached production. The same model was also to have been sold as the BSA Fury, with a few cosmetic changes.

Early version of the 3TA engine unit with skew gear drive to the camshaft and distributor. Fortunately it seems to have been realized that this form of gearing is not well suited to driving such items as camshafts, with their odd and cyclic loading. But the essence remained for the points for some time.

The original machine was designed by Edward Turner and a prototype built. It had an all-alloy engine with inclined cylinders and gear-driven, twin overhead camshafts built in unit with a four-speed gearbox. Inside went a 180 degree crankshaft, so the pistons no longer rose and fell together, which dictated the twin carburettors and separate exhaust systems. Coil ignition was used with a twelve-volt system and the duplex primary chain went on the right.

The gearchange and kickstart pedals were on the left, and the unit went into a light frame with a single downtube. This had pivoted fork rear suspension and new front forks with external springs. The front wheel had a disc brake with mechanical operation, but the rear was a drum; both rims were of 17 in. diameter. The result was quick, and timed at the MIRA proving grounds at 112 mph, but had many problems. The frame and forks were too light for the job so the handling was poor, while the front brake tended to seize. Worse still was the engine which broke its crankshaft with ease.

The whole machine underwent a massive revamp before it was announced to the public late in 1970. The basis of the engine remained the same with inclined cylinders and 180 degree crankshaft, but most else was altered in one way or another. The two camshafts were chain driven from a slave shaft geared to the left end of the crankshaft, and ran within chambers cast into the sides of the head and barrel.

The primary side remained on the right but a five-speed gearbox was installed and there was provision for an optional electric starter. Carburation was by twin Amal Concentrics and the road version retained the two exhaust pipes with low-level megaphone silencers. There was also to be a street-scrambler model, and for that both pipes ran to the right at waist level where there were two silencers, one above the other.

The cycle parts were also changed, so the engine unit went into a frame with duplex tube loops. This had the slimline forks common to the range for 1971, and also the conical hubs front and rear. In this form the machine was far more likely to have succeeded, but was one of the casualties of the financial trauma the group suffered at that time so only a handful of machines were made.

The firm also tried an overhead camshaft on the 500 twin in the early 1950s, with a chain drive on the right of the engine. This had a Weller tensioner, which gave trouble due to the long chain run, and on test the engine seemed to be down on power. It was later found that the cam timing was not correct, but by then Turner no longer supported the project which was thus abandoned.

Other 350s

Long before the Bandit there had been an economy 350 which would have revived the

New Imperial name if it had gone into production. It was built just after the war as the 3TU to indicate a utility machine for the commuter market.

The engine was a vertical twin with upright valves moved by pushrods in tubes behind the block. This extended down to include the top half of the crankcase, in car practice style, with just an alloy sump beneath it. A one-piece head with separate rocker box was used, with the single carburettor at the rear and twin exhausts at the front feeding into one silencer low down on the right.

The timing side had a train of gears up to the rear camshaft and the dynamo behind the block. A car-type distributor for the coil ignition was driven from the train and angled forward from the timing chest, which also contained the oil pump of the dry sump lubrication system.

The transmission was much like that of the prototype TRW, so was a separate unit with three speeds. It and the engine went into a rigid frame with undamped telescopic front forks and ran on 15 in. disc wheels with 4 in. section tyres. These were retarded by drum brakes and shielded by a deeply valanced front mudguard and total enclosure of the top half of the wheel at the rear. The finish was all-black for economy, but on test the machine proved slow and the engine overheated. Triumph did not proceed with it.

Another 350 was an early version of the 3TA, which was not too far removed from the final model although it differed in appearance. This was because there was no timing side, in the normal Triumph sense, as the camshaft was placed fore and aft on the engine centre line and high up in the crankcase from where it operated the tappets and valves much as usual.

This was not, in fact, a new notion for the firm. They had used the same location in a 1913 twin-cylinder engine and for that the two shafts were connected by skew gears. In the more modern machine a chain drove a cross-shaft from the left end of the crankshaft, and skew gears then drove the camshaft and distributor. This engine also had a gear oil pump in place of the normal twin-

The Triumph 200 cc two-stroke twin built around 1957, which used the Cub gearbox and its cycle parts to produce a model for experimental tests. It was soon dropped, for the Triumph name stood for four-strokes and they had no real knowledge of the other variety.

plunger type, but the skew gears wore rapidly, as they do under load, so the engine was modified to the normal Triumph layout. In this form it became the 3TA and all the unit models that followed it used the same layout.

Small two-stroke

Triumph was always seen as a four-stroke firm and they generally were, but toward the end of the 1950s they did build a two-stroke which was also a twin. It is thought that this was in response to rumours of the Ariel Leader, which appeared later, and it is likely that Triumph would have been aware of this since both firms belonged to the BSA group.

The two-stroke was only of 200 cc capacity and was unusual in that there was only one casting each for the block and head. Induction was direct into the crankcase via reed valves, and the exhaust ports were well splayed out. The engine was attached to the transmission of a Tiger Cub and fitted to a rolling chassis for a mobile test, but was soon dropped as a project.

Larger side-valve twin

This was a 750 cc twin based on the TRW, with a view to producing an engine suited to sidecar use. At the time this aspect of motorcycling was quite popular and much served by 500 cc side-valve singles, since the demise of the prewar vee-twin.

While based on the TRW, the 7ST, as it was known, did differ in a number of respects. The crankshaft continued to be clamped up, although of greater stroke, and the iron block and alloy head served both cylinders. The greatest change was to the timing gear, where the single front camshaft was driven by a duplex chain and its left end drove another shaft via skew gears. This ran back in a casting to a distributor with an auto-advance, while the oil pump drive remained at the end of the camshaft.

One engine was built into the then-current cycle parts and run on the roads, but was felt to be wanting. The testers found the performance inadequate with a bare 70 mph top speed, so the firm stuck with the Thunderbird and offered sidecar gearing for it.

A second engine found its way onto the market many years later, in the mid-eighties, and this was installed into cycle parts from the 1950-54 period. Thus, this machine has a rigid frame, sprung hub, four-bar tank and nacelle. It runs well and opinion is that it would work well with a sidecar.

Other prototypes

There are more prototypes known to have survived which can come onto the market or be referred to in some way or another. Often they were merely development stages

The enlarged version of the TRW was this 7ST which retained the side valves and was tested in this form in 1987. When built, it was intended for sidecar use. But the days of the large-capacity side-valve engine ended in the 1930s, so this one was far too late.

that an engine or machine would go through to prove a point, so many no longer exist. Such is the way with development models in all spheres, and most are worn out anyway by the time they have done their job.

One of the Triumphs was simply an engine, not intended for motorcycle use at all, but a 700 cc inline four built as a heavy-duty generator for the RAF. It was based on two 3T top halves on a suitable crankcase and was mounted in a cradle to allow it to be moved around as needed.

Another, at the other end of the scale, was a 50 cc moped powered by a Puch engine in a steel-beam frame with cantilever suspension and known as the TR50. It was built in 1977 at a time when the NVT group was involved with the Easy Rider moped.

There were twin-cylinder engines built in the mid-seventies with a balancing piston placed in the front of the crankcase. If seen, the lump in the casting is obvious but does not confirm the presence of the special crankshaft within, unless this too can be inspected.

Falling into the prototype class was the batch of ten T100D machines that awaited completion when the Meriden sit-in began in September 1973. These differed in having a disc front brake, alloy forks, conical rear hub and silencers from the larger twins. Both US and UK styles were built, high bars and change of tank finish being the main differences. One or two of the batch were later completed.

Prospects

Ratings are impossible to work out for this class of machine, but generally four or five stars would be awarded for any genuine ex-works prototype. Authentic models will be well documented and easy to confirm, but the others will come with evasive comments and should be avoided at all costs.

The same applies even more so to works specials, as it is all too easy to claim that the machine was ridden by a works rider at some time. Full checks are needed on this and contemporary photographs may well assist you in your research.

In general, steer clear of these models if you simply want a Triumph to rebuild, ride and maybe show. These machines are more for the in-depth, totally committed Triumph owner whose heart still lies in Meriden. They are also for museums, where we can all enjoy looking them over. Often that is best for both the machine and us.

Chapter 9

Cafe racers and customs

Specials are the machines and parts that are neither standard-build Triumphs nor proto-types or works specials. In any case, there are many of them and the Triumph buyer needs to be able to pick through the many possibilities and variations to recognize the good from the bad.

Specials come in many forms and usually involve another make of frame and cycle parts—or major alterations. Options in this

A typical Triton built in a stark form with no frills. This one was intended for fast road work, with no nonsense about ease of use in town or any-thing else. It shows all the characteristic fea-tures of the type with no concessions.

case are not the ones that Triumph listed but items made by others for the marque. These can range from a finned rocker box cap to a big-bore kit, special primary drive or new frame.

Cafe racers

Cafe racers are normally built by individuals to meet their requirements, but some are professionally prepared to a greater or lesser extent. They come in many forms but the most common is the Triton, with the Triumph engine in Norton featherbed cycle parts and a gearbox from either make.

Standards of construction vary a great deal and the best of these machines makes a superb motorcycle; however, the worst are too dangerous to ride at all. Therefore a careful inspection of what is being offered is essential, as is having a prior idea as to what type of machine is wanted, including its main fittings, and just what it is to be used for.

One of the first to produce the Triton commercially was Dave Degens who ran Dresda Autos. His machines are always well made. They normally carry a make label and tend to be in the classic format with 650 cc engine, and are little removed from the racer-with-lights concept.

There were other Triton builders and most sold parts as well, so many machines were built up in home workshops using these. Any of the twin engines could be

The Hyde Harrier triple of 1987, which shows how a company can create a special machine to meet the customers' demands. Nice use of the upright Trident engine in a good chassis with fabricated wheels. Quick and a trifle noisy.

Custom work of the highest standard, with intricate engraving on the engine cases and immaculate finish. This type of machine is far from the classic mainstream, but at its best represents just as much dedication and skill as any other area.

used, as could any Norton featherbed frame. The early Tritons often used a complete Manx Norton, less engine and gearbox, as a basis, for there was a regular supply from the Formula 3 car world in the early 1950s. When this dried up the builders turned to road machines for their source of parts, and while some used the twin frame, more seem to have been based on that from the 350 cc single.

Many other makes of frame have been used to create specials over the years with Benelli, BSA, Dot, Ducati, Greeves, Honda, MV and NSU all playing their part. Often the forks, wheels and other details were collected from a variety of sources which varied over the years. In one era it was common practice to fit an Italian front hub, always with drum brake, but later on it was easier to find a Japanese component. These became plentiful as machines for road or racing switched to discs which have no place on a cafe racer.

Custom built

This is Harley-Davidson territory, where the ride is laid-back and casual for boulevard cruising or covering the long, straight highways of the American Midwest. From this concept came the Low Rider theme with stepped two-level seat, highway footpegs up near the front of the engine, small tank, raised bars and extended forks.

In the extreme, these trends led to the chopper with the features, especially the extended forks, taken to "way out" and the finish and detailing to suit the owner. Some are crude but others are skillfully made and artistically finished.

The main alternative to the Harley for many years was the Triumph twin. It was easy enough to find the basis in a junkyard, and for many the rigid frame was preferred, as the hardtail was the accepted norm for most owners. Since so much of the machine would be discarded or modified drastically, the use of a secondhand or crashed machine saved both money and time.

Once the Japanese had seen that the custom motorcycle was more than a fringe section of the market, they responded with their own ideas on the matter. To the true believer, however, you either have the real thing in the shape of a Harley-Davidson or build your own which invariably seems to mean a Triumph twin base.

Engine options

There have been many engine options over the years and it is quite common to find one or more on any standard Triumph. Less usual will be the more exotic kits such as the eight-valve head, but in some circles this will be considered an advantage.

A number of items were mainly cosmetic and in this class come the finned points cover, sump plate and rocker box cap. This last item was always a popular line with dealers, as the twin was prone to losing caps and the finned ones were preferred by many owners. Another option with fins was an exhaust pipe clamp; although the standard items were finned, the options had bigger ones.

For more serious work there were the big-bore kits, and one of the best known of these was and is the Morgo. This took the 650 engine out to around 740 cc, or up to 770 cc on maximum oversize. A new iron block was the main item in the kit along with new pistons and head gasket, so the conversion was easy enough to carry out. As with all such work the general engine condition could have a major effect on the final result, and the real benefit came only if the bottom half and cylinder head were up to the mark.

Nourish Racing Engines, or NRE, also do a big-bore kit but in their case offer an alloy block with iron liners to open the engine to 686 cc. The block will also accept their eight-valve head, which is generally preferred to the Triumph head used on the TSS or the Weslake one that that was based on. An alloy block with Nikasil bore treatment for the 750 cc twins appeared in the mid-eighties from Les Harris, who was also making the complete machines at that time.

NRE also produced many other engine parts including special crankshafts, connecting rods and camshafts, as did Mick Hemmings and Norman Hyde. There were a large number of other engine details availa-

All too often a chopper represents backyard engineering with crude work and doubtful machine strengths. This one is unusual in having the side-valve TRW twin engine rather than the more normal ohv one, but has the stock hardtail and extended forks. The first gives a hard ride when combined with the low-mounted and unsprung saddle, while the second is too weak for its own or the rider's good.

ble from these and other sources, including various improvements to the lubrication system.

These items are more likely to be found in the engine of a cafe racer and most, except for big-bore blocks, cannot be detected without taking some of the engine apart. The parts may also be found in machines of an innocuous appearance, although this is less common. In some cases it may be a matter of a wolf in sheep's clothing, or simply because the parts were on hand when needed.

In most cases it will not matter much if the engine has some nonstandard internals, with two provisos. One is that they do not make the machine impossible to use as you intend to use it. The other is more subtle, and concerns the balance of one part against the other. It is necessary for components to work well together to produce a harmonious result. This will make the machine much nicer to ride while, if the balance is not there, riding the machine will be hard work and therefore tiresome to use.

This machine was offered as a competition prize and is a 1971 type with the new frame and conical hubs. It has been given a custom finish which is mainly plating, so not as extreme as the total custom or chopper styles, but is still different from the stock model.

Chassis options

There may be even more chassis options, but for a start there are a number of belt primary-drive conversions available for most of the twins. These may retain some of the existing clutch or not, but where the belt runs dry there can be a lubrication need for the clutch bearing.

There are options for the clutch itself and these range from detail improvements such as a radial needle roller in the pressure plate to a radical change to hydraulic operation. There are also special clutch plates, and further into the transmission is the five-speed gearbox which can be an original Triumph or one from Quaife.

Wheels and brakes are another area full of option possibilities that could offer a conversion to twin-leading shoes, disc brakes, alloy rims or cast alloy wheels. Some of these will complement the machine but others may detract from the overall effect, so machine

Perhaps the most popular engine option for the Triumph twin after playing with the camshafts is the big-bore block. These have been available for many years in various capacities and in iron or alloy. This one has nine studs and is typical of the type.

This is a nice combination of the twin engine and the Hurricane styling, which combine to make a machine that could have come from the factory. The alloy wheels certainly do not look out of place and go well with the tank and seat moulding.

The style of the Rob North frame, which was used by the racing triples and set a form seen on many other machines. It is classic in its elegant joining of headstock to rear fork pivot, which is essential to hold them true on road or track.

One of the many Rickman Metisse frame kits with associated engine plates, pipes and other fittings. This one is for the pre-unit engine, but others held the unit twin of either size and there were more for other makes. All were finished to the same high standards—the business!

use may dictate whether the change is good or bad for you, the buyer.

The front forks are less likely to have been changed, other than for a cafe racer or custom model, but the rear units may easily be nonstandard. This can be simply because the originals wore out and something better was chosen as the replacement.

Finally there is the frame itself, and in addition to the featherbed and others from different makes there are those built specifically for the marque. One of the best known is the Rob North frame used by the works Tridents, but there are many more for both twins and triples. All offer something, and a modern frame can complement the older engine well.

Often the frame is part of a complete kit which will usually include much-improved front forks and modern rear units. There may be cast or alloy wheels to go with the better suspension, and invariably disc brakes to keep the machine in check in modern traffic.

To go with the update of the base-line cycle parts, there will also be more cosmetic items such as fuel and oil tanks, cockpit fairing, seat moulding with tail unit and mudguards. These may be available by themselves in a whole host of styles or as part of the frame kit, which can fully modernize the engine and gearbox package.

The Les Williams Legend has already been mentioned. Another is the Harrier, produced

Rickman also built up complete machines to customer specification and their same high standards, with this one a Metisse for desert use. It is fitted with the 649 cc unit Triumph engine which in turn could be well worked on to improve its performance.

by Norman Hyde, with a Harris frame. Such machines and others enable the Triumph enthusiast to adapt his or her machine to cope with today's road conditions and result in a fine, fast motorcycle that offers all that is best on two wheels.

For off-road use—or on—one of the most respected names is that of the Rickman brothers who, disillusioned with stock scrambles models back in the 1950s, built something better. In doing so they created their Metisse with Triumph twin engine, and from this came a range of parts, frame kits and complete machines. These were for all forms of motorcycling, and most of the road kits were in the cafe racer form.

In time they produced a range of parts, frame kits and complete machines with the frames always distinguished by their nickel-plate finish. They were also all-welded with duplex construction, except for the top tube, and the pivoted fork was designed with an eccentric at the pivot for chain adjustment. The frame was surmounted by a nice petrol tank whose lines ran back into the seat unit and tail. This last could be short for scrambles or a little longer for the road while the whole assembly was set off by side panels which could house an air cleaner and carry the competition numbers.

The parts range became extensive in time with many of the details made to suit the frame kits. Thus, there were engine plates, mainly to suit the various Triumph twins, exhaust pipes for the same, footrests, mudguards and much more. In later years there

The Dresda frame and cycle parts as offered by Dave Degens in 1970 as the basis for many a Triton. He was still building them two decades later when they were as popular as always and just as effective. He returned to the race circuits to promote them and showed he had lost none of his skills.

Paul Dunstall included many special parts for the Triumph in his range, although he was far more associated with Norton twins. The tank, seat, bars, rearsets and swept-back exhaust pipes seen here show his high working standards which applied to all parts for any marque.

were other machines, other engines and a good deal of quality fibreglass equipment such as fairings, panniers and top boxes, but it is for the frames, especially with a Triumph engine, that the Rickmans are best remembered.

They were also involved with the Weslake eight-valve conversion for the Triumph engine and with Dave Degens, producing the Dresda-Metisse. The latter continued with his own Dresda frame as well; this was similar to the featherbed but altered in minor ways. Other parts for both engine and chassis were also offered by Degens who continued with his frame into the classic bike revival era.

Paul Dunstall was another who did not neglect the Triumph although his name is normally associated with Norton. This did not stop him producing a whole range of parts for the Meriden models. All names to conjure with and the machines are highly desirable to collect, ride and appreciate in money and aesthetic terms.

Electric options

Again, there are many of them and some can be essential for a machine in daily use. While the concours specialist will always keep all parts original, few will deny that twelve-volt electrics, a halogen headlight and a monster rear light are really essential on the roads these days. For the engine a change to electronic ignition is often a good move.

The Greeves frame was strong and large enough to take a range of engines other than the usual Villiers, and is here seen with a Cub working hard in a trial. The small unit twin also went in easily and a number of these appeared, usually for road use.

The ignition side of the later models is easy enough to alter and riders have several choices. A capacitor system powered by the alternator and fired by the points allows the machine to run without a battery which can be useful with some models. Leading on from that are points-assisted systems where electronics take the current so the contacts are long lasting. And then come full electronics from Boyer or Mistral with magnetic triggering. There are also firms who can offer a trigger head to replace a magneto and in some cases to build it into the magneto body to retain the original appearance.

The generating side may also be uprated, whether dynamo or alternator, and the conversions provide for a twelve-volt system and usually more power. While this may still be below that of a modern machine, it can be a considerable improvement, allowing the use of better lights and a more reliable generator output control system.

Prospects

The question you have to ask yourself is whether any option is an asset to you and a feature you require on your machine. If it is not then its additional value to you is nil, regardless of its first cost.

Classify and summarise the options to check whether they are performance, comfort, reliability or convenience oriented and compare this with your needs. Look for a balance and for how the options have been incorporated and work together. If the package is harmonious then the result will be good but all too often it is not, so the options became a debit when talking money with the owner.

Complete packages such as the Rickman are always well rated and highly collectable. The actual rating may vary more than with standard models and depend on originality of the specialist parts, their condition, and the fashion and style of the moment. Any complete Rickman or Dresda model has to rate four stars but as machines for a long term investment or short term gamble. They are not models likely to stay static financially so be prepared for the market to be more volatile and for their value to rise or fall over the months. In the long term they must be good but at times you will have to hang on and wait for them to climb back up after a fall or depressed period. This could take a year or two but will happen.

All will be nice to have and ride in the meantime in the sure knowledge that they will be worth more next year.

A street scrambler Rickman Metisse, which is rare in being fitted with the smaller unit Triumph twin engine. The engine size no doubt dictated the monster rear sprocket. The silencers and lights are enduro style, as is the bodywork with its race plate mouldings. A good tool for the job.

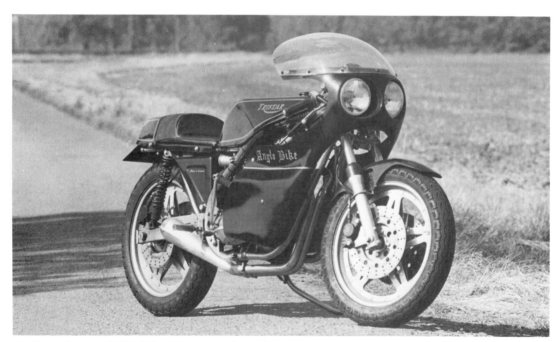

Another nice special build with any number of extras for the discerning rider. Among them are the North-style frame, race-type tank and seat, fabricated wheels, box section rear fork, twin headlamp fairing and all those well-executed details that combine so well.

Scooters

The Triumph company had two attempts at the postwar scooter market—one in liaison with BSA—but neither was any sort of a success. The machines were too late and not quite what the market wanted. Scooters had to be light and lively as the Italian models

The Tigress scooter model TW2 with twin-cylinder engine but no electric start, as deduced from the exhaust tailpipe at the rear and lack of second battery box on the apron. Here it is on show at Earls Court, but on the road was prone to overheating and failed to make its expected impact on the market.

were if they were to sell well, and their whole philosophy was different to that of the motorcycle.

By the time Triumph reached the marketplace, not only was their timing off—the good days were about to slide away—but they also lacked an understanding of the fickle market. Their product was not launched until late 1958 and comprised a three-model range in Triumph or BSA colours and badges.

Scooters

The smaller model had a 172 cc engine based on the BSA Bantam, but the others used a more complex 249 cc ohv twin with either kick or electric start. This latter engine was really too large for most scooter owners who mainly kept to the 200 cc class and one cylinder.

From the clutch onward the two models were the same, and the engine of the smaller one copied the Bantam but only in design as few parts were identical. It was a basic two-stroke with no complications but the air cooling was assisted by cowling the top half, and a fan attached to the flywheel magneto on the right.

The mainshaft extended to the left to carry the clutch, and this drove back via spur gears to a four-speed gearbox. Internally this was much like that of the Cub and retained the positive stop mechanism but controlled by two pedals, one for up and the other for down.

From the gearbox a duplex chain drove to the rear wheel with a slipper tensioner, as the centres were fixed. The drive was totally enclosed in an alloy case which also acted as the pivoted arm for the rear suspension. The arm swung from the main engine and gearbox casting about the output sprocket, so the wheel movement had no effect on chain tension.

The twin-cylinder engine was based on one major alloy casting for block, crankcase and gearbox shell. The crankshaft was a one-piece forging and drove the rear camshaft by gears. The head was in alloy with the valves in a line, although the outer exhausts angled out from the centre, so the rockers were positioned to suit. Ignition was

by points and coil, so the right crankshaft end carried an alternator which had both cooling fan and a starter gear ring. Lubrication was by wet sump and a single-plunger pump driven by the camshaft.

From then on the twin was the same as the single and the power unit plus final drive went into the usual form of tubular frame. It differed from most in that the headstock

The later 100 cc scooter with automatic transmission but not a great seller. It came too late and had too many "motorcycle" minor controls for the novice rider to set or adjust when starting, so rather missed its market.

tube was bolted to the two apron downtubes and the front forks were single-sided with both spring and damper in the solitary left leg. At the rear went a single-suspension unit and thus both wheels went on stub axles and were 10 in. diameter pressed-steel types with 5 in. drum brakes. Bodywork was conventional scooter and the list of accessories was extensive. These were always important to a scooter dealer, for they could bring as much profit as the complete machine and more could be added later for a happy customer.

The model range had its glamourous launch with celebrities in attendance, but then came the dawn. The scooters failed to find many customers, for they had rather missed the boat and the right class. But the firm kept them in the range for a while. There were few changes other than in colour options, and late in 1964 the twins were dropped with the single running on only to the next summer.

This range was not the firm's only attempt to capture the scooter market. In 1962 they launched another aimed at the mass market. This elusive idea of a cheap machine sold in large numbers had been the downfall of many firms, and it was the Honda step-through that finally met the bill. The new Triumph, sold as the Tina, was another that did not.

The scooter used a 100 cc two-stroke engine laid flat with a vee-belt transmission to the rear hub assembly. The belt gave the effect of a clutch and automatic ratio changes, so control was essentially simple with just throttle and brakes. Unfortunately there were also other minor controls for the rider to cope with and a start/drive switch to use before moving off. This was a safety device that cut the engine if the rider speeded it before ready to move off. The Tina was a small machine and ran on 8 in. wheels on stub axles. Suspension was by rubber at the front and a spring unit at the rear, while the bodywork was in the normal scooter style.

The model failed to catch on to any extent and during 1965 was renamed the T10. This had some cosmetic changes, and the safety switch went under the seat where the rider's weight operated it while the front brake lever was moved to the left handlebar. All this made little difference and although the model hung on till 1970, it was in a declining market and it was long gone by the time the seventies boom arrived. And a good thing, said most people.

Prospects

I've given two stars to the twins and one to the rest. Few people ride, collect or restore old scooters, although there is a club, so the market base is small indeed. Since there is little interest, to most people they are neither a good ride nor a good investment.

The Tina and T10 barely scrape up one star between them, for they have curiosity value only. A scooter enthusiast might have one to complete a collection, but would ride something else. So if you like them, you're on your own.

The Tigress range is a trifle more interesting, but in that case it has to have the twin engine, preferably with electric start and plenty of accessories. The TS1 may be rare but that is about all that can be said for it.

Chapter 11

★★★ 1991–1992 Daytona 750 and 1000
★★★ Any 1991 model
★★ All other models

Hinckley Triples & Fours

In 1983 the Triumph name was bought by successful businessman John Bloor who had plans to revive the marque. These plans did not include taking the press into his confidence until he was good and ready, and his security was such that even speculation finally died away for want of any hard facts or even rumours.

What did become known as an intention to create a new factory on a 'green-field' site at Hinckley, between Leicester and Coventry. The building work was carried out by another of Bloor's firms so there was no news from that quarter, other than that it would be equipped with the best in computer-controlled machining centres and robotic welders.

There was some speculation as to whether the Phoenix design might be used but that was quickly examined and discarded. Then the team went to work and steadfastly ignored all questions and queries; it was 1988 before any clues emerged. This came about when some engine castings where shown at a convention in the USA, suggesting modern three- and four-cylinder, in-line, watercooled engines in sizes ranging from 750 to 1200 cc.

It was September 1990 before the new range was launched at the Cologne show, the press having a preview and sight of the factory in June that year. Before then there was speculation based on the castings that had been seen, photographs of the engine unit and some of unmarked models out on test.

There were six machines in the range, all with much in common in both engine and chassis. Nothing of the design came from Triumph's past, it being modular in conception and modern in construction. The factory mirrored this, being equipped with the latest in technology for its machining, welding and quality control. All who were shown around the plant were impressed—this was a serious undertaking.

The basic Hinckley engine in its four-cylinder form and showing its clear-cut lines. Camshaft drive on right; triple is essentially the same.

The most popular model and engine proved to be the Trident and the 900 triple, this being the 1992 version. Much of the cycle side is common to the range.

One of the sports-tourers was the Trophy 1200 with the larger four-cylinder engine. Nice machine and nice lines for 1992.

The Speed Triple was introduced for 1994 in a classic café style and is here in its 1996 black finish, the alternative being orange.

The Adventurer was introduced for 1996, based on the Thunderbird and styled for the American cruiser market; this is the 1997 version.

The engine design was modern, but not exceptionally so. A transverse, in-line row of cylinders, inclined forward a little, water-cooled and having twin overhead camshafts and four-valve cylinder heads. Four capacities were available, two as triples and two as fours, but all based on a common 76 mm bore. This enabled the combustion chambers, valve sizes and much else to be common throughout the range.

Strokes varied at 55 or 65 mm so that the triple's capacities were 748 or 885 cc. With the extra cylinder they became 998 or 1179 cc, compression ratios being 11.0:1 for the short-stroke engines and 10.6:1 for the long-stroke ones. All had one 36 mm Mikuni carburettor per cylinder and ran on unleaded petrol.

Engine construction was based on a horizontal crankcase joint, the top half of the casting being combined with the cylinder block, which was fitted with wet liners. A one-piece cylinder head carried the two camshafts, which were chain driven from the right-hand crankshaft end, the chain running up through a tunnel; it could be changed without removing the cylinder head.

Internally, there was a one-piece crankshaft, balancer shafts to reduce vibration, wet-sump lubrication and gear primary drive on the right. The triples had one balancer shaft ahead of the crankshaft, the fours had two balancers. An elaborate breather system dealt with emission problems and reduced crankcase pressure to inhibit oil leaks. A cartridge oil filter was fitted to the underside of the crankcase whereas the trigger for the electronic ignition went on the right-hand

Daytona 1000 of 1992, top of the range and fitted with the smaller four-cylinder engine and fairing with twin headlamps. Bigger brakes to match the performance.

crankshaft end. Both the generator and starter were mounted behind the block, above the six-speed gearbox, which was in unit with the engine. Final drive was by chain on the left.

As at least two models were to be produced without any form of engine shield, the complete unit had a style and line of its own. This differed both from the past and from Japanese or Italian multis to give the new Triumph its own form. Power outputs varied from 90 to 141 bhp with alternatives to suit the restrictions of some countries. All were adequate with good mid-range torque.

The major cycle parts were common throughout the range, the engine being a stressed frame member and hung from the tubular spine frame. Kayaba 43 mm telescopic forks went at the front while rear suspension was of the rising-rate type, controlled by a single Kayaba unit. The rear fork had eccentric chain adjusters built into the wheel spindle ends.

Triple-spoke, cast-alloy wheels were used, fitted with Nissin disc brakes. At the front there was variation, the roadster and sports-tourer models having twin 296 mm discs and twin-piston calipers, the sports models fitting twin 310 mm floating discs and four-piston calipers. All had a single 255 mm disc for the rear wheel but the sports models fitted the caliper and its torque arm under the rear fork; the others had it above. Tyre sizes also differed.

Fixtures and fittings were typical of the late-1980s: modern, but not excessively so. The result was a strong and individual line and style that suited the marque's niche in the market.

The six models comprised three pairs, each pair offered with a choice of engines. The most basic were the Trident 750 and 900 roadsters, both with three-cylinder engines and without any fairing. The strong lines of engine, tank and side panels made a good visual impact, enhanced by the finish in

Tiger 900 off-road model, new for 1993 and on show at the NEC late in 1992. While using much from the range, there were a good number of changes to suit the style and use.

British racing green or metallic gun-metal grey, and black.

Next came the Trophy 900 and 1200 sports-tourers, these equipped with a fairing and powered by three- or four-cylinder engines. Colours were basically grey or black with side flashes in silver or red. Finally there were the Daytona 750 and 1000 sports models, again with three- or four-cylinder engines and fairing. In their case the fairing line was more sporting and it carried twin round head-lamps in place of the single, rectangular unit used by the Trophy. Colours were red, blue or grey with more extensive graphics. All models had a revised tank badge based on the original but sharpened up to give a more modern edge.

The range had a good reception and the firm still enjoyed much goodwill, the public keen to see the new machines with the old and hallowed name. It was April 1991 when the first models reached the showrooms and September before all six models were available, but it was soon clear that Bloor's team had done well. There were a few early problems but these were rectified quickly and there was no doubt that quality was the watchword.

Road tests soon showed Triumph had got it right. The machines compared with the best while retaining their own image. Not as sharp as some of the race replicas but for general use this was no bad thing. Smooth, low-down grunt in plenty, good handling, good brakes and acceptable fuel consumption.

Little had to be altered for 1992, the range remaining unchanged but in revised colours. This had begun during 1991 when both Trophy and Daytona machines on road tests had been finished in red with silver stripes. For 1992 the Trident models were in metallic British racing green, metallic Cherry red, or two-tone metallic Cherry black. The Trophy models had the choice of Lancaster red, metallic Caribbean blue or metallic charcoal grey, plus British racing green for special edition anniversary models. The Daytona models were in Lancaster red or Assam black, while a pannier set became available for all as an option.

By April 1992 it was possible to see the sales pattern which showed the 900 triple to be by far the most popular engine. Half the sales were Trophy models, most of the other half were Tridents, and the majority had the 900 engine. Only 10% of the machines sold were Daytona models whereas over three-quarters of the buyers specified the 900 triple engine.

Some colours were revised at the same time, the Trophy being available in metallic Oxford blue, Burgundy red, Charcoal grey or British racing green, the Caribbean blue remaining available. The Trident and Daytona

Trident Sprint 900, new for 1993, having a cockpit fairing and twin headlamps in Daytona style.

The Trident engine in its 1993 black finish and showing its strong lines.

750 colours stayed as before, but the Daytona 1000 changed to radiant red as the only choice.

In the Autumn 1992 news of the 1993 models began to filter through. The Trident and Trophy models would continue with minor changes, the two Daytona models would be replaced by two new versions, and there would be two new models, one a trail machine and reviving the Tiger name.

Changes for the Trident amounted to more chrome-plating, a black finish to the engine and exhaust pipes, lower seat height and footrests, and a two-tone finish. This was in British racing green, Cinnabar red or Diablo black with a contrasting tank panel.

For the Trophy models there were the changes to lower the seat and footrests, revised mirrors, a digital clock, higher handlebars and black-chrome exhaust pipes. The Trophy 1200 was fitted with the larger 310 mm floating front brake discs and four-piston

calipers while the colour choice became Caspian blue, British racing green or Candy apple red, the engine, frame, wheels and seat being in grey.

New was the Trident Sprint 900, a version fitted with a half fairing carrying twin round headlamps and finished as for the other Trident models.

The Tiger 900, a SuperMoto/Enduro model, used a detuned version of the triple engine giving 85 bhp but with more mid-range torque. It had a strengthened frame, wire wheels, radial tyres, extended wheelbase, long-travel suspension, longer seat and a half fairing fitted with twin round headlamps. The wire wheels were fitted with either a 110/80x19 or 100/90x19 in. front and a 140/80x17 in. rear tyre, while the brakes were twin 276 mm discs at the front and thus smaller than the other models. The rear 255 mm disc was stock. There was a sump guard, and initially, a problem in the UK over the

The Daytona 1200 at its launch at the NEC late in 1992, the new top-of-the-range model.

fitment of a plastic petrol tank. Colours were sandstone, Caspian blue or Pimento red, the engine being in black but with the engine covers coloured to match the machine. The raised three-into-two exhaust was finished in black.

The replacement Daytona models were the 900, using the triple engine, and the 1200 which had a 147 bhp version of the four. Both had slimmer rear panels and lower screen, retained the twin round headlamps, had the silencers raised and were fitted with a single seat hump. The engine, frame, forks and wheels were finished in black while the colours were Pimento red, Racing yellow or Barracuda blue metallic.

The whole range went forward for 1994 with many detail improvements and two additions, both powered by the 900 triple engine. One was the Speed Triple that took the classic café racer style without fairing and was finished in a choice of colors set off by white-faced instruments in a traditional twin-clock mounting. Unlike other models, it was fitted with a five-speed gearbox.

The second new 1994 model was the Daytona Super III that had a tuned, 115bhp engine of reduced weight but with six speeds, six-piston front brake calipers and new 17-inch wheels. Carbon fibre was used for the mudguards, silencers and fairing inner panels.

The new 1995 Thunderbird revived a name from the 1950s. It used the five-speed 900 triple, while the format was that of the classic roadster, right down to the grill tank badges as used from 1957 to 1965, wire-spoke wheels, and short, tubular silencers from a bygone era. There was no fairing, the instruments and headlamp were individual as in the 1960s, and even the engine covers were revised and polished to help create a true and most successful cruiser.

The two 1996 Trophys were given new bodywork that included twin headlights in the latest style as well as panniers as befitted a high-class tourer. The Speed Triple went over to the six-speed gearbox while the Thunderbird had a new, oval-section, aluminum rear fork.

The new Adventurer was based on the Thunderbird but styled more for the American market in an easy-to-ride cruiser format. It kept the 900 triple power plant with five speeds, but adopted high-rise bars, a single seat, the tank badge as used by Triumph twins from 1966 to 1968, raked forks, megaphone silencers, and a ducktail rear mudguard. A host of factory accessories were listed.

For 1997, the Daytona 900, Daytona Super III, and Speed Triple were replaced by the Daytona T595 and the T509 Speed Triple. The radical Daytona T595 broke new ground for the firm in many areas. The new engine remained a triple with a 65 mm stroke, but the bore went up to 79 mm and the capacity to 956 cc and was designed in collaboration with Lotus Engineering. It kept the twin camshafts and four valves, but lost weight and went over to a computer-controlled engine management system and fuel injection. The result was 130 bhp at 10,200 rpm.

The engine and its six-speed gearbox went into a new perimeter frame using oval-section aluminum extrusions and fitted with a single-sided rear-suspension arm controlled by a Showa unit. At the front went 45 mm Showa forks, the wheels were a Triumph design cast by Brembo, and the dual front discs had four-piston Nissin calipers. A sleek fairing was fitted and carried twin headlights, the result a super-sports model able to run with the best.

The second new model was the T509 Speed Triple that kept the existing triple engine but uprated it with fuel injection to 108 bhp at 9,100 rpm. The chassis came from the T595, with its single-sided swingarm, forks and brakes, but the style was lean and bold without a fairing so the twin headlamps sat side by side under the instrument panel. In its new form the Speed Triple had street fighter style and was the lightest model in the 1997 range.

Prospects

With the success of Hinckley there are plenty of machines on the market so their value falls in line with other moderns. The early Daytona models were only built for two years so will become rare, but the others less so. Any from the first year could become collector's items for that reason alone.

Chapter 12

Locating and buying

Buying any motorcycle is a process of location, viewing and negotiation, best done in that order. At all stages the more you know, the better the situation will be regardless of what you are buying or from whom. A crisp remark that some feature cannot be original can work wonders for your self-confidence, but only if you have the data to back it up should your bluff be called.

Tact may also help, since some owners will not take kindly to any suggestion that their masterpiece could have feet of clay. Thus, the owner's temperament should be gauged first while asking about the machine's history—or you could find yourself in the street. With the more desirable models, some owners definitely will sell only to what they see as a good home for their machine,

This is a page from the 1951 catalogue showing the sporting TR5 in its original style but with the diecast head and barrel. The new head meant a change to the siamesed exhaust pipes, but the remainder of the machine stayed as it was and continued to offer its abilities.

Enthusiasm for road racing can take many forms and is shown here by A. Crocker, who entered this prewar 5T in the 1947 Senior Clubman's TT in the Isle of Man. Nothing about entry, travel or practice can have been easy. He retired after three laps but no doubt still enjoyed his ride.

and set themselves up as judge and jury. As demand usually exceeds supply, there is no way round this if you want the machine, but invariably the owner will respond to your enthusiasm.

Your needs

Before you try to locate your Triumph you should first decide which one you want and what you will use it for. Sounds obvious, but all too often a machine is bought on impulse and within weeks is found not to fit the new owner's needs, wishes or pocket. It's much better to think it out first, even though many of the factors may conflict and chance can always bring the unexpected.

Your needs, if you intend to ride the machine on a daily basis, are a good deal different than if you wish to exhibit at shows. Between these two extremes are weekend use, regular rallies or occasional

rides, and all place varying demands on the machine.

Anything approaching regular use suggests that you will need to sacrifice originality for better brakes, lights, tyres and suspension. All can be altered without losing that typical Triumph line, and for many owners this gives a most desirable result. They finish up with the marque they desire but updated and amended to use modern technology to keep pace with modern traffic. This is very much a philosophy from the postwar era, when it was a common practice for machines to be modified to improve them, update them or simply adapt them better to their owner's need.

In some cases the changes became major, with the Triton the outstanding example which combined the Triumph engine with its ready supply of tuning parts with the Norton featherbed frame. The result became a classic in its own right and revived again in the 1980s.

The Triton reflects one builder's personal needs, so that in any form it can be regarded as being in original condition. Not so a standard model, and to the restorer and concours exhibitor original fitments are all-important. With the rapid growth of the classic movement this has brought its own set of problems, for some parts that turn up are new-old-stock (NOS) and thus genuine even if ancient. Others are reproduction parts and their quality can vary greatly. If they go on the inside they may affect reliability, while if external they will alter the appearance. Carburettors, exhaust systems, tank rubbers, footrest rubbers, transfers and tyres are all items that wear or deteriorate so are likely to need replacement. Somehow, to the experienced eye, reproduction parts always look to be that, even in a photograph.

Your intended use will indicate the model and era that you should seek, but this is always subject to what you can afford. For many of us this may mean an adjustment, and we have to settle for a Cub or a 3TA rather than the Bonneville or Trident we crave. Once you have gotten over the initial disappointment, you'll realize it's better to own a machine you can really afford than one that is stretching your resources to breaking point.

The amount you spend to purchase the machine is never the end—there are always further costs with any motorcycle. How much depends on the condition of the machine and the alterations you plan to make. A no-expense-spared restoration job can run into a large sum if you farm out the work, and a sizable one even when you do much of the work yourself. Do not take on more than your workshop or abilities can cope with, and do not delude yourself on this point. If you do, you can easily pull apart the machine and get stuck, then find you cannot afford the services of a specialist and have to dispose of the resultant basket case at a loss. Set your sights at an attainable level and accept that you may not have the facilities or skills to do it all. Few of us have.

All this must be taken into account, and you should plan to leave yourself enough money after the purchase to cover tax, insurance and any needed work. The latter will always come to twice your estimate.

Research

Before you start hunting for your machine, find out as much about it as you can. You are holding a good deal of what you

The Triumph factory in 1974 during the sit-in, with so many machines going nowhere. Standing idle for so long cannot have done them much good, and it is doubtful whether the engines were turned over during this period.

need in your hand right now, so read it *before* you go shopping, not afterward. That way you can be assured you are getting the best buy for you.

It is important that you keep this last point in mind and buy for *your* needs and not someone else's. Ignore them and concentrate on you, for if you are happy with your machine, it is of no account what others may think of your choice.

Add to your knowledge by checking prices for both private and dealer machines, with notes on the machine condition. As you will soon learn, they come in many forms ranging from the bare bones at an autojumble swap meet up to a concours restoration job bought from a dealer. Machines may be original or not, complete or not, shabby, rusty or partly restored. They can be badly restored

which may be worse, as a poor exterior job can indicate untold horrors under the covers.

Build up your store of knowledge on this so you can begin to make a reasonably accurate assessment of most models and conditions. That way you should buy at the right price unless you let your heart rule your head. Fight this, if you can, so you at least keep to a sensible price if not the best one.

Locating the machine

The possible sources are dealers, small advertisements in local papers and specialized magazines, auctions, local and one-make clubs, autojumbles and personal contacts. All need to be followed up especially if you are after a rare model. Machines such as the early TR5 seldom come onto the market.

Nice line of Thunderbirds as supplied to the Fiji police in 1956. Once the Speed Twin was established as the London police motorcycle, many other forces both at home and abroad followed suit and adopted the twin for patrol work.

The USA dealer school at Baltimore in 1958, with Jack Wickes from Triumph in charge. Such visits and the courses all helped to keep the machines well serviced and dealer morale high.

As a result, Triumph sold a lot of motorcycles and had a profitable business. Would that this had continued . . .

Long line of Triumphs outside H&L Motors of Stroud in Gloucester in 1960. The firm was a main dealer for the marque for many years so

had an extensive background on the twin and Cub models. Note the many inducements to buy, following the best sales year ever, 1959.

Most already have a queue of potential buyers who have asked the owner for first refusal.

The expensive solution is a dealer who specializes either in Triumphs or vintage and classic machines. These days you are not likely to find a machine at a general bike shop at anything less than the going rate, and often it will be higher than usual because the dealer has heard vaguely that all such machines are now worth real money.

Triumph motorcycles went all over the world but this one just has to be a little special. If you can find the Thunderbird that was inside the packing case it would have to be worth that extra money, but proving it could be hard.

Small advertisements present two problems. One is that the worthwhile ones always seem to be a long distance away, and the other is establishing the real condition before you set out on the journey. All too often what the owner has given a glowing description turns out to be too rusty, too incomplete or too poorly restored to make it a good proposition.

Even if you have travelled all day, the golden rule is to keep your money in your pocket unless you really are happy with what is on offer. We have all done the opposite more than once, but invariably pangs of regret will set in halfway back home or soon after the mistake is installed in your garage.

In this circumstance it may be worth making a "silly" offer. Before you open your mouth, make two positive decisions. One is to ask yourself if you want the machine at all, even if it was free. Do not kid yourself that "it will be handy for spares" because it won't. All the parts you are likely to need because your main machine is in trouble will also be worn out, split or otherwise useless.

It is possible that the offering may have parts on it that you could use, but allow only for the price of those parts and nothing else. Remember, they are bound to need some repair and maybe repainting.

The second decision is the amount at which to pitch your silly offer. Decide on two figures, with the first your offer and the second the figure you will actually go to on barter. If the owner says no way to your offers, just drive home and start hunting again.

Auctions can offer a wide selection of machines and their condition. You can look, read the description in the catalogue, but you can't run the engine. Check carefully that the machine corresponds to its description and really is what you seek because there is no going back. Listen to the auctioneer at the start to establish sales conditions and if there is a buyer's premium. Decide on your limit before the auction starts, write it in the catalogue and stick to it regardless. If the machine fails to reach its reserve, seek out the owner, if you can, to see if you can strike a deal. After all, he or she will not have to pay commission and can hardly wish to trail the model back home again.

The local club is unlikely to provide much of a selection of machines but could give you a bargain if one happens to be what you are after. Make sure both you and the seller are interested in dealing, though. If the seller is hesitant but you're not, the deal could cost you more in the long run. The one-make club may be a better bet. There will be more on offer with the chance of finding some nice machines at the right price and with a decent history behind them. The Triumph

club in the United Kingdom produces its own magazine entitled *Nacelle* and this can be a good source of machines and parts.

Autojumbles and swap meets can be a source of complete machines, but be extra careful, for again there is no going back. Most machines on offer are tired and well worn, often with a fair number of items missing. Some will have engines that do not match their frames, and internals not belonging to their externals. Occasionally you will find a machine that is original, essentially complete and worth considering. The

This is the works 3T ridden by Jim Alves in the early postwar era. He is seen here in 1947 and was one of the few who could ride a twin suc-

cessfully in trials. The engine had revised valve timing, small carburettor and progressive throttle action using a device under the tank.

This is just the sort of machine to avoid no matter how cheap it is. The frame and forks are from other makes, so none of the cycle parts will be of any use while the engine internals are suspect and could be from anything. Might be worth giving up garage space for if the engine unit is free—but unlikely.

stall holder will know what it is worth so there will not be much room for bargaining, but always make the attempt.

Most purchases at autojumbles are parts or assemblies, but even these need some careful checking. It is for these that I wrote *Triumph Twin Restoration*, with its up-to-the-elbows detail. Check, check and check again, and someday you may find a swan under the rust and grime—but not often. More likely it says T120 on the case but is a Thunderbird within.

Personal contacts can be best of all. In some cases they may be the only answer for the rare models, so the more you have, the better your chances. While perseverance is fine, always remember to keep to the right side of the fine line between keeping in contact and becoming a nuisance and a bore.

Even trickier is the situation where the owner, usually a man, dies to leave a widow with a desirable machine. It is hardly proper

English Prime Minister Harold Macmillan and US President Dwight D. Eisenhower on the Strand in London during a 1959 visit. They are flanked by police on Triumphs, who practiced their job at the Crystal Palace racetrack around less costly cars.

etiquette to make your bid at the graveside, but fatal to wait too long or another will succeed in your place. The matter of price can also be awkward, for the widow may not know or care as to the machine's value. Often a son, close relative or friend will take charge of the disposal of the machine and other relevant items. This at least makes it easier to conduct business.

Basket cases

These are best left alone unless you know a great deal about Triumphs in which case the warning is superfluous. In theory, the various boxes shown to you contain one complete motorcycle dismantled into its component parts. In practice, the machine may have been incomplete even when the parts were together.

It is far more likely that the parts come from more than one model, often other marques as well, and will never make a complete machine. There are exceptions but they do not occur too often and the trick is to recognise one when it comes. It is also usual for the parts to be well worn and often the boxes represent a clear out from a garage or workshop where the owner has had a series of similar models and what is on offer are the discards.

Basket cases can better be viewed as a box of spares which may be useful and must be priced accordingly. Even where the seller is

Nice restoration of an early 3T at a rally in 1980. Not concours but all there and in good order so an easy way into the classic movement. Then, the revival of interest in older machines was just getting under way, but now the model is rare and worth a good deal more.

quite genuine about the machine and its history it is all too easy to forget items that were missing or broken or lent to a friend. Keep well clear unless you are certain or have an expert to advise and assist with the deal and the assembly.

Viewing the bike

Some people have this down to a fine art and, with a few well-chosen phrases, imply that they are doing the seller a favour by removing the machine and really ought to be paid for this kindness. Most of us find the going harder but with any classic it is an essential stage.

The job depends greatly on the condition of the machine in the general sense, as this sets the standards to be looked for. A machine with rounded nuts, dull paint work, dangling cables and unkempt air is unlikely to be mechanically perfect inside, so should be judged on that basis. A decent exterior usually implies that the interior is similar, and also that it is correct for the model. Even where the outside has been spruced up in an attempt to mask an indifferent condition, it is usually fairly easy to spot this with a little practice. There will be too much polish on the main covers, none in the recesses and not enough correct settings and adjustments.

The parameters to use when viewing depend on the use to which you will put the machine, as has been discussed already. Do not forget these or you could end up with the wrong machine at the wrong price. However, whether the machine is for daily riding or weekend showing, the state of completeness, correctness and condition all count. The degree to which they count will vary according to use, but in all cases a nice machine is worth having and a wreck is always a wreck.

There are basic inspection checks to be made when looking over any machine with a view to buy, and these apply regardless of model, originality or type, so need to be carried out always. Start with the overview, to assess whether it is more or less all there, the general condition and whether it still excites—or produces a feeling of dread. If it's

Triumph was always prepared to build something special if a customer ordered enough, but this had to be based on the standard machine such as this TR7 of the late 1970s. Details altered included the single seat and rear carrier, both of which were easy to fit near the end of the production line.

A 1983 T140 built to police specification for the South Yorkshire force. It had radio, extra lights including a flashing blue one, panniers, fire extinguisher and full-size fairing. Police forces preferred the Triumph as long as it was backed by good spares support and reliable operation.

the latter, then say farewell and go on your way. You will never be happy with it even after an expensive rebuild.

Next check it in detail from stem to stern. Inspect the tyres, try to rock the wheels and feel how they turn, look for play in front and rear suspension, see if the headstock is tight or loose once the damper is slack and check the suspension for movement, noise and damping.

Look over the cycle parts for splits and cracks, as these will need welding and then refinishing. See if there are dents in the tanks, since these could be expensive to correct; inspect the underside of the petrol tank for signs of leaks or attempts to mend same. See if the brakes work at all and whether the spokes need replacement. Check the controls and switches to see if they work easily and correctly or are either stiff and corroded or sloppy and worn out.

Finally, check the engine and gearbox. Look over both for oil leaks, signs of excess jointing compound and cracked or broken fins or lugs. See if the chains are in good order and adjustment, and then ask the owner to start up the machine. If there is a refusal or a feeble excuse, either be on your way or drastically revise your opening offer. There is no reason why any Triumph should not start easily and run nicely. Learn how they sound before you go shopping, and allow for an all-alloy engine to rattle only a little more than an iron one.

Expect a crunch when the owner puts it into first gear, even if the clutch has been freed off. After that, though, the drive should take up smoothly and the gears

147

should change quickly and easily. If the owner refuses to do this, either there is a gearbox problem or the clutch needs attention.

If you have the chance to ride the machine on the road, or be a passenger, expect it to run in a happy manner. They normally do, so if you find one that does not this indicates a need for some adjustment as a minimum, and maybe some major work. Even if it is only a matter of a minor correction, the fact that the seller has not bothered is a clear indication of attitude.

Identification

In addition to the general checks, there are more specific ones, as well as paperwork, which come together in some cases. Start with the engine and frame numbers which *must* be taken from the machine and *must* be checked against those shown in the registra-

tion documents. In the United Kingdom this is called the V5, and if one is not forthcoming it may well be that the machine is not registered and not entitled to the number plate it carries.

These numbers must be checked promptly or there could be problems in the future. In the United Kingdom, if there is no V5 you will have to apply for one, with proof of ownership of the machine and a dating letter to confirm the age of the model. If all is well, it will then be issued with an age-related mark; if not it will receive a number with a letter Q prefix. Either will devalue it to a degree in its home country where the original number is often held in high esteem, but procedures in other countries differ.

The next stage is to compare the numbers with those given in the appendices of this book, bearing in mind that the model year

The Tiger Trail or Adventurer TR7T of 1981 on show with high-level exhaust system. This differed from others seen on the model, and was one of several attempts to broaden the range while keeping the same basic major assemblies.

runs from the previous August. Thus a 1955 model, for example, could be built, sold and then registered in November 1954. From 1969 the firm used a code system to date the models, and the two letters give both month and year. Be careful with these because again they run from August to July, and the second letter (year) functions over this model year.

The above tells you what the machine *should* be, but you need to confirm that it is what it claims to be. For this, you use the identity charts given in the appendices to check out the external features for the model in question. If any one is not there, or not as it should be, look through the charts to see which model it has come from. Where necessary refer also to the general text, but in most cases the chart should cover all that you can inspect of a complete machine.

The internals are another matter, but if the outside checks out there is a good chance

that the interior will also. However, always remember that it is only too easy to change around parts in the twin so be extra careful with the sports models. Not that it is all that desirable to find T120 cams in a 6T. The all-iron engine may well protest, as will an iron head on a real T120.

One further check can be the finish and colours, which are also given in the appendices. The patina of age on an original finish can be detected quite easily, as can a new coat of paint. If the colours do not check out, this may not be too serious but it is another factor to take into account with your overall assessment.

If the machine is not all standard, you have to decide how important this is to you, which will depend on your intended use. For general riding it will not matter much and the changes may well be desirable improvements. If you are going to show the machine, however, they can be more important and in

This is a 1980 T140ES with electric starter which is housed in the old magneto position behind the engine. It drives into the timing chest via gears and thus the covers are unique to the model to enclose these.

this case a judgement has to be made as to the effect and the ease of correction. Some detail parts may be simple enough to replace with originals but others could prove impossible.

Negotiations

These can be ultra-short or protracted. It may be a case of a price without negotiation or a conversation that continues for months before a deal is finally struck. Fortunately, for most of us the middle course prevails and an equitable price is arrived at without too much delay.

There is no negotiation in the normal sense at an auction, where you have to decide on your limit and stick to it. Only if the machine fails to reach its reserve are you likely to be able to do a private deal.

When buying from a dealer or a private owner there will normally be a stated asking price. This may be viewed as a starting point and represents the highest value the owner has dared to pitch without losing all response to his ad or whatever. This may state that the price is not negotiable, but most are, especially when faced with a pile of crisp bank notes.

Just as the asking price is the highest that the seller hopes to get, so your first offer is the lowest you are going to buy at. Think long and hard before coming out with a figure, for it will be nearly impossible to reduce it later. The only chance of this is if some undisclosed fact comes to light during the discussion. But even this will not do much to strengthen your position.

First ask yourself whether you really want the model, whether it fits your needs and if the one you are looking at is the right machine. It may be fitted with a number of options which the seller will claim greatly enhance its value and, while this may be true, they only count if you really want

The Speed Triple was revised for 1997 to become the T509 with a new chassis, more power, and less weight.

them. Thus the optional sprung hub could become a defect if you really want a machine with rigid frame.

If you finally decide that you have found just the machine for you, then run down your notes for faults to criticize and features that are nonstandard or unwanted. Work out the figure you could be happy at and then go down to your first silly offer.

This may be greeted with derision, but it is a start and the ball is now with the seller who can either say no way or suggest another figure. Keep at it, but remember that you may not be alone in reading these words!

The deal

All being well, you should arrive at a price with the seller in due course. This may involve a trade-in with a dealer, although this is less usual with the older machines, and your calculations must take all this into account.

Once you have paid for the machine it is your responsibility, which means you need to insure it. Even if you do not intend to ride

A Bandit on show in its final form when the public showed much interest—but it was not to go into production. Leaving the keys in place was a big mistake, even with the machine on a plinth, as trade and press were unlikely to resist the temptation.

it on the road immediately, you should cover it against fire or theft. It will be best to go to a specialist broker who can arrange coverage on an agreed value basis to reflect what the model is worth. The coverage for road use may also be on a restricted mileage basis, which will be more suited to the use that most owners will have.

When you pay, do get a receipt that details the machine, registration mark and engine and frame numbers. Also, in the United Kingdom, collect the V5 and MoT documents, if there are any, and any other material on the machine such as parts list, owners handbook or instruction manual. Check that they are relevant to the model and year. If not, they will need replacement.

The next problem you will face is to transport the machine home, since you can ride it only if all the documentation is in order and you have your riding gear with you. Often it will mean using a van or a car and trailer unless the seller can assist.

The golden rule

If you are not totally happy about the machine, leave it to someone else and walk away. Make sure you now what "totally happy" is for you, regardless of others' opinions, machine value or investment rating. If the machine really is the one you want, then buy it and enjoy it to the full, whether Trident or Tina, Bonneville or Cub.

Happier days on the Triumph stand at Daytona in 1958 when the 3TA was new and the Bonneville soon to appear. There were problems after that, but the Turner twin was to continue for another 30 years, with some famous victories along the way. It remains as the most popular model on the classic motorcycle scene.

152

Engine and frame numbers

More than one system was used for the various Triumph models and thus these are dealt with in turn. In most cases, the engine number has the model code as a prefix while the frame may have this or simply a letter T to indicate Triumph or nothing at all. Some engines may carry additional letters such as P for police or C for high compression, but these are not part of the normal numbering system. Norton featherbed frame numbers are included in this section for the benefit of potential Triton owners.

Prewar singles and Page twin

Year	Model	Engine number	Frame
1934	6/1	1V4	
1935	6/1	1V5	
1936	6/1	1V6	
	T70	T1L6	L
	T80	T2T6	SI
	T90	T5S6	SII

1937-40 For all models the engine had the model code as a prefix plus a year number such as 7, 8, 9 and 40 to cover the years concerned, and then the serial number.

Twins for 1938-49

For these models the engine had the model code as a prefix plus an indication of the year in the form of the last one or two digits of the year. Generally the prewar models will have an 8 or 9, and the postwar ones a 46, 47, 48 or 49, but this is not always so and the single figure may be found on some postwar motors. The prefixes used were T or 5T for the Speed Twin, T100 for the Tiger 100, 3T for the 350 twin and TR5 for the Trophy.

Postwar engine numbers commenced for each year as follows:

Year	Engine number
1946	72000
1947	79046
1948	88782
1949	100762

Frames are less easy to judge, but prewar they were prefixed TH for the 5T model and TF for the T100. Postwar the markings were TC for the 3T and TF for the 5T, 6T, T100 and TR5, but the numbers do not match those of the engines.

Twins for 1950-69

A new system was introduced with just the model code as the prefix and the serial number. The 1950 models have a letter N suffix, and from 1951 to 1952 they have an NA suffix. The smaller unit twins all have a letter H prefix, while the 650 engines in duplex frame have a letter D and the unit models have the letters DU as prefixes.

Year	Engine number for unit 350 & 500 cc	Engine number for Pre-unit 500 & 650 cc
1950		From 100N
1951		101NA-15808NA
1952		15809NA-25000NA, then 25000-32302
1953		32303-44134
1954		44135-56699
1955		56700-70929
1956		70930-82799, then 0100-0944
1957	H101-H760	0945-011115
1958	H761-H5484	011116-020075
1959	H5485-H11511	020076-029363
1960	H11512-H18611	029364-030424, then D101-D7726

Year	Engine number for unit 350 & 500 cc	Engine number for Pre-unit 500 & 650 cc
1961	H18612-H25251	D7727-D15788
1962	H25252-H29732	D15789 on
		Unit 650 cc
1963	H29733-H32464	DU101-DU5824
1964	H32465-H35986	DU5825-DU13374
1965	H35987-H40527	DU13375-DU24874
1966	H40528-H49832	DU24875-DU44393
1967	H49833-H57082	DU44394-DU66245
1968	H57083-H65572	DU66246-DU85903
1969	H65573-H67331	DU85904-DU90282

Year	Engine number
1955	23323NA-23597NA
1956	23598NA-25447NA
1957	25448NA-27127NA
1958	27128NA-27175NA
1959	27176NA-27346NA
1960	27347NA-27645NA
1961	27646NA-28185NA
1962	28186NA-28464NA
1963	28465NA-28827NA
1964	28828NA-28986NA
1965	28987NA-29605NA

Singles, twins and Tridents for 1969-83

During 1969 a new coding system was introduced using a two-letter prefix for the month and model year, followed by the model type code and machine serial number. In the letter code, the first letter was for month and the second for model year, which ran from August of the previous calendar year to the following July. From July 1980 a letter A was added to the existing two to enable the system to continue, and was used for the larger unit singles, twins and triples. The letters were used as follows:

Letter	Month	Model year
A	January	Aug. 1978-July 1979
B	February	Aug. 1979-July 1980
C	March	Aug. 1968-July 1969
D	April	Aug. 1969-July 1970
E	May	Aug. 1970-July 1971
G	June	Aug. 1971-July 1972
H	July	Aug. 1972-July 1973
J	August	Aug. 1973-July 1974
K	September	Aug. 1974-July 1975
N	October	Aug. 1975-July 1976
P	November	Aug. 1976-July 1977
X	December	Aug. 1977-July 1978
KDA	1981 models	Sept. 1980-Apr. 1981
EDA	1982 models	May 1981-Jan. 1982
BEA	1983 models	Feb. 1982-Jan. 1983
T140V AEA34393		Last model Jan. 21, 1983

The first new machines of a new model year may start before August and thus carry an earlier prefix letter for the month, so be careful of this system.

TRW twins

Year	Engine number
1950	14401N-14459N
1951	6044NA-14320NA
1952	22001NA-22838NA
1953	22839NA-23273NA
1954	23274NA-23322NA

Singles

Year	Engine number	Model
1953	101	T15
1954	101	T15, T20
1955	8518	T15, T20
1956	17389	T15, T20
1957	26276	T20, T20C
1958	35847	T20, T20C
1959	45312	T20, T20C
1960	56360	T20, T20S
1961	69517	T20, T20T, T20S/L
1962	81890	T20, T20S/S, T20S/H, TR20, TS20
1963	88347	T20, T20S/S, T20S/H, TR20, TS20
1964	94600	T20, T20S/S, T20S/H, TR20, TS20
1965	99720	T20, T20S/S, T20S/H, TR20, T20SM
1966	101	T20, T20S/S, T20S/H, TR20, T20SM
1967	—	T20S/C
1968	—	T20S/C

Scooters

Year	TS1 Engine	TS1 Frame	TW2 Engine	TW2 Frame
1959			W101	101T
1960	S101	4001	W3201	4001T
1961	S6720	18801B	W11790	18800T
1962	S11407	30140B	W17800	30140T
1963	S12498	31825B	W18485	31825T
1964	S13263	33661B	W19793	34286T
				(last)
1965	S13576	34300B		
Last		34468		

TW2S engines with electric start have letter E suffix

Devon twins

An easier system was used for these machines, with two letters followed by the serial number for each year in turn. The original prototype was broken up, but all the others were sold and are out in the marketplace. The numbers were used for the Bonnevilles and Tigers as they came off the line.

Year Engine and frame number
1985 FN000002-FN000191
1986 GN000192-GN000788
1987 HN000789-HN001176
1988 JN001177-JN001258 (built March 9, 1988)

Norton featherbed frames

These first appeared in 1952 when the sub-frame was bolted to the main loop, but from 1955 it was welded in place. In 1960 the frame was modified to pull the top rails in closer, and this became known as the slimline and the earlier type as the wideline. The frame number should be stamped on the left rear fork pivot gusset plate, with the year letter and model number at the top and the serial number in a vertical line beneath this. The number can be composed of two or three parts, with the model year letter (used up to 1960), the model code number and the serial number.

The codes were as follows:

Year	Letter	Code	Model
G	1952	4	ES2
H	1953	10	International 40
J	1954	10M2	Manx 40
K	1955	11	International 30
L	1956	11M2	Manx 30
M	1957	122	88
N	1958	13	50
P	1959	14	99
R	1960	18	650
		20	Atlas

Hinckley models

Hinckley VIN start numbers by model and year.

Model	1991	1992
Trident 750	0000870	00002423
Trident 900	0000964	00002430
Trophy 900	0000785	00002407
Trophy 1200	0000011	00002455
Daytona 750	0000872	00002445
Daytona 1000	0000326	00002436

1993 VIN start number is 4902
1994 VIN start number is 9083

Model features

The model range charts list the years each model was built and the external features, providing a check list for when viewing a potential purchase. Engine and frame numbers remain the first point to check *always*. After examining them, the features can give a good indication as to whether the machine is what it says it is, or if it is from another year or a hybrid.

The list of features for each model was first developed in an attempt to isolate a unique set for each year, as a basis for checking. Many items appear for several models, as they were common to the range. The list was then expanded to include points that are often of interest, even though they may not help with dating. This may mean that for one particular year there are several points that changed, but all are included since all changes should have been made if the machine is original.

All the features listed are external and can be checked without dismantling. The internal changes are of no help when you are just looking over the machine, but remember that on the twins they may be far-reaching due to the ease with which parts may be switched around. When going to view, make a list but also take along this book. It will help you establish where any rogue parts have come from.

Model range years are also covered in the rating box at the start of most chapters, and list the production year rather than the calendar year. The new season's models were built from August on to be ready for the November show and distribution to the dealers, hence the distinction.

Prewar models
6/1
No real changes from 1934–36

Singles		Model year			
Feature	'36	'37	'38	'39	40
T90 2-port head	*				
high toolbox	*				
chain stay toolbox		*	*	*	*
new gearbox		*	*	*	*
central rear lamp			*	*	*
Bakelite panel			*	*	*
front plate surround				*	*

Pre-unit models
3T		Model year				
Feature	'46	'47	'48	'49	'50	'51
tank panel	*	*	*			
nacelle				*	*	*
4-bar badge					*	*
headlamp flat	*					
headlamp domed		*	*			
sprung hub		*	*	*	*	*
through bolts	*	*	*			
block studs			*	*	*	* (from engine 89333)

5T Model year

Feature	'38	'39	'46	'47	'48	'49	'50	'51	'52	'53	'54	'55	'56	'57	'58
6-stud block	*														
girders	*	*													
mag-dyno	*	*													
dynamo			*	*	*	*	*	*	*						
alternator										*	*	*	*	*	*
tank panel	*	*	*	*	*										
4-bar badge							*	*	*	*	*	*	*		
grill badge														*	*
bayonet tank cap								*	*	*	*	*	*	*	*
Amal 6 carb	*	*	*	*	*	*	*	*	*	*	*				
Monobloc												*	*	*	*
headlamp flat	*	*	*												
headlamp domed				*	*										
nacelle						*	*	*	*	*	*	*	*	*	*
underslung pilot									*	*	*	*			
Slickshift															*
dual seat opt							*	*	*	*	*				
ext. drains	*	*					*	*	*	*	*	*	*	*	*
big main												*	*	*	*
sprung hub				*	*	*	*	*	*	*	*				
S/A frame												*	*	*	*
full-width hub														*	*

6T Model year

Feature	'50	'51	'52	'53	'54	'55	'56	'57	'58	'59	'60	'61	'62
4-bar badge	*	*	*	*	*	*	*	*					
grill badge							*	*	*	*	*	*	
Amal 6 carb	*	*											
SU carb			*	*	*	*	*	*	*				
Monobloc										*	*	*	*
big main			*	*	*	*	*	*	*	*	*	*	*
alloy head												*	*
2-1 exhaust													*
dynamo	*	*	*	*									
alternator					*	*	*	*	*	*	*	*	*
sprung hub	*	*	*	*	*								
S/A frame						*	*	*	*	*			
duplex frame											*	*	*
bathtub											*	*	*
full-width hub							*	*	*	*	*	*	*
8 in. front brake												*	*
underslung pilot			*	*	*	*							
Slickshift									*	*	*	*	

T100 Model year

Feature	'39	'46	'47	'48	'49	'50	'51	'52	'53	'54	'55	'56	'57	'58	'59
girders	*														
mag-dyno	*														
tank panel	*	*	*	*											
4-bar badge					*	*	*	*	*	*	*				
grill badge													*	*	*
dual seat std							*	*	*	*	*	*	*	*	*
alloy engine							*	*	*	*	*	*	*	*	*
big main									*	*	*	*	*	*	*

T100

Model year

Feature	'39	'46	'47	'48	'49	'50	'51	'52	'53	'54	'55	'56	'57	'58	'59
sprung hub		*	*	*	*	*	*	*							
S/A frame										*	*	*	*	*	*
Amal 6 carb	*	*	*	*	*	*	*	*	*	*					
Monobloc											*	*	*	*	*
headlamp flat		*	*												
nacelle					*	*	*	*	*	*	*	*	*	*	*
underslung pilot							*	*	*	*					
Slickshift														*	*
8 in. front brake										*	*	*	*	*	
vented front										*	*	*	*		
full-width hub														*	*

T110

Model year

Feature	'54	'55	'56	'57	'58	'59	'60	'61
alloy head			*	*	*	*	*	*
Amal 6 carb	*							
Monobloc		*	*	*	*	*	*	*
dynamo	*	*	*	*	*	*		
alternator							*	*
underslung pilot	*	*						
Slickshift					*	*	*	*
4-bar badge	*	*	*					
grill badge				*	*	*	*	*
duplex frame							*	*
bathtub							*	*
vented front	*	*	*	*				
full-width hub					*	*	*	*

TR6

Model year

Feature	'56	'57	'58	'59	'60	'61	'62
dynamo	*	*	*	*			
alternator					*	*	*
duplex frame					*	*	*
trail m/c	*	*	*	*	*		
road m/c						*	*
high exhaust	*	*	*	*	*		
low exhaust						*	*
2–1 low pipes							*

Unit models

3TA

Model year

Feature	'57	'58	'59	'60	'61	'62	'63	'64	'65	'66
tool pad	*	*	*	*						
bathtub	*	*	*	*	*	*	*			
outward tub flange				*	*	*	*			
skirt								*	*	
distributor	*	*	*	*	*	*	*			
timing case points								*	*	*
primary tensioner					*	*	*	*	*	*
2–1 pipes							*			
sports front guard									*	*
bolted frame strut								*		
welded frame strut										*
18 in. wheels										*
eyebrow tank badge										*
12–volt electrics										*

5TA

Model year

Feature	'59	'60	'61	'62	'63	'64	'65	'66
tool pad	*	*						
bathtub	*	*	*	*	*			
outward tub flange	*	*	*	*				
skirt						*	*	
distributor	*	*	*	*	*			
timing case points						*	*	*
primary tensioner		*	*	*	*	*	*	*
2–1 pipes					*			
sports front guard							*	*
bolted frame strut						*		
welded frame strut								*
18 in. wheels								*
eyebrow tank badge								*
12–volt electrics								*

T120

Model year

Feature	'59	'60	'61	'62
nacelle	*			
dynamo	*			
alternator		*	*	*
duplex frame		*	*	*

TR5

Model year

Feature	'49	'50	'51	'52	'53	'54	'55	'56	'57	'58
square fins	*	*								
Amal 6 carb	*	*	*	*	*	*				
big main						*	*	*	*	*
Monobloc							*	*	*	*
Slickshift										*
S/A frame						*	*	*	*	
full-width hub									*	*
4-bar badge						*	*			
grill badge									*	*

TR6

Model year

Feature	'56	'57	'58	'59	'60	'61	'62
4-bar badge	*						
grill badge		*	*	*	*	*	*
Slickshift			*	*	*	*	
7 in. front brake	*						
8 in. front brake		*	*	*	*	*	
full-width hub			*	*	*	*	*

158

T90

Feature	'63	'64	'65	'66	'67	'68	'69
grill badge	*	*	*				
eyebrow badge				*	*	*	
frame badge							*
Monobloc carb	*	*	*	*	*		
Concentric carb						*	*
skirt	*						
2–1 pipes	*						
bolted frame strut				*			
welded frame strut					*		
new frame					*	*	*
12–volt electrics				*	*	*	*
chaincase access cover						*	*
finned heat sink						*	*
no rear unit covers						*	*
tls front brake							*
exhaust balance pipe							*

T100A

Feature	'60	'61	
bathtub	*	*	
tool pad	*		
375 carb	*		
376 carb		*	
cutout button	*	*	
coil ignition		*	(from engine H22430)

T100SS

Feature	'62	'63	'64	'65
distributor	*			
timing case points		*	*	*
skirt	*	*		
2–1 pipes	*	*		
2–2 pipes			*	*
frame strut				*

T100

Feature	'66
eyebrow badge	*
welded frame strut	*
Monobloc	*
12–volt electrics	*

T100S

Feature	'67	'68	'69	'70
eyebrow badge	*	*		
frame badge			*	*
Monobloc carb	*			
Concentric carb		*	*	*
chaincase access cover		*	*	*
finned heat sink		*	*	*
no rear unit covers		*	*	*
tls front brake			*	*
exhaust balance pipe			*	*
case breather				*
seat grab rail				*

T100T

Feature	'67	'68	'69	'70
eyebrow badge	*	*		
frame badge			*	*
2 Monoblocs	*			
2 Concentrics		*	*	*
chaincase access cover		*	*	*
finned heat sink		*	*	*
no rear unit covers		*	*	*
8 in. front brake		*	*	*
tls front brake			*	*
exhaust balance pipe			*	*
case breather				*
seat grab rail				*

T100R

Feature	'66	'67	'68	'69	'70	'71	'72	'73	'74
eyebrow badge	*	*	*						
frame badge				*		*	*	*	*
welded frame strut	*								
Monobloc	*								
2 Monoblocs		*							
2 Concentrics			*	*		*	*	*	*
chaincase access cover			*	*		*	*	*	*
finned heat sink			*	*		*	*	*	*
no rear unit covers			*	*		*	*	*	*
8 in. front brake			*	*		*	*	*	*
tls front brake				*		*	*	*	*
exhaust balance pipe				*		*	*	*	*
case breather						*	*	*	*
seat grab rail						*	*	*	*
turn indicators						*	*	*	*

T100C

Feature	'66	'67	'68	'69	'70	'71	'72
eyebrow badge	*	*	*				
frame badge				*		*	*
ac ignition	*						
2–1 pipes	*						
single silencer	*						
welded frame strut	*						
Monobloc carb	*	*					
Concentric carb			*	*		*	*
chaincase access cover			*	*		*	*
finned heat sink			*	*		*	*
no rear unit covers			*	*		*	*
tls front brake						*	*
exhaust balance pipe						*	*
case breather						*	*
seat grab rail						*	*

TR5T

Feature	'73	'74
oil-in-frame	*	*
slim forks	*	*
conical hubs	*	*
2–1 exhaust	*	*

6T

Feature	'63	'64	'65	'66
skirt	*	*	*	
grill badge	*	*	*	
eyebrow badge				*
6-volt electrics	*			
tdc timing slot			*	*

TR6

Feature	'63	'64	'65	'66	'67	'68	'69	'70
grill badge	*	*	*					
eyebrow badge				*	*	*		
frame badge							*	*
2-1 exhaust	*							
6-volt electrics	*	*	*					
tdc timing slot			*	*	*	*	*	*
Monobloc carb	*	*	*	*	*			
Concentric carb						*	*	*
chaincase access cover						*	*	*
tls front brake						*		
bellcrank tls brake							*	*
exhaust balance pipe							*	*

TR6R

Feature	'66	'67	'68	'69	'70
eyebrow badge	*	*	*		
frame badge				*	*
Monobloc carb	*	*			
Concentric carb			*	*	*
chaincase access cover			*	*	*
tls front brake			*		
bellcrank tls brake				*	*
exhaust balance pipe				*	*

TR6C

Feature	'66	'67
eyebrow badge	*	*
Monobloc carb	*	*
waist-level pipes	*	*

T120

Feature	'63	'64	'65	'66	'67	'68	'69	'70
grill badge	*	*	*					
eyebrow badge				*	*	*		
frame badge							*	*
6-volt electrics	*	*	*					
no inlet balance pipe	*							
tdc timing slot			*	*	*	*	*	*
Monobloc carb	*	*	*	*	*			
Concentric carb						*	*	*
chaincase access cover						*	*	*
tls front brake						*		
bellcrank tls brake							*	*
exhaust balance pipe							*	*

T120R

Feature	'63	'64	'65	'66	'67	'68	'69	'70
grill badge	*	*	*					
eyebrow badge				*	*	*		
frame badge							*	*
6-volt electrics	*	*	*					
no-inlet balance pipe	*							
tdc timing slot			*	*	*	*	*	*
Monobloc carbs	*	*	*	*	*			
Concentric carbs						*	*	*
chaincase access cover						*	*	*
tls front brake						*		
bellcrank tls brake							*	*
exhaust balance pipe							*	*

T120C

Feature	'63	'64	'65
waist-level pipes	*	*	*
6-volt electrics	*	*	*
no-inlet balance pipe	*		
tdc timing slot			*
grill badge	*	*	*

T120TT

Feature	'64	'65	'66	'67
grill badge	*	*		
eyebrow badge			*	*
tdc timing slot	*	*	*	

T120 Thruxton

Feature	'65
fairing	*
rearsets	*

TR6R

Feature	'71	'72	'73	
oil-in-frame	*	*	*	
conical hubs	*	*	*	
push-in exhaust pipes	*	*		(from XG42304)
single rocker lids	*	*		(from XG42304)
disc front brake		*		

TR6C

Feature	'71	'72	'73	
oil-in-frame	*	*	*	
conical hubs	*	*	*	
undershield	*	*	*	
push-in exhaust pipes	*	*		(from XG42304)
single rocker lids	*	*		(from XG42304)
disc front brake		*		

TR6RV

Feature	'72	'73
oil-in-frame	*	*
conical hubs	*	*
five-speed	*	*

TR6RV

Feature	'72	'73	
push-in exhaust pipes	*	*	(from XG42304)
single rocker lids	*	*	(from XG42304)
disc front brake		*	

TR6CV

Feature	'72	'73	
oil-in-frame	*	*	
conical hubs	*	*	
five-speed	*	*	
push-in exhaust pipes	*	*	(from XG42304)
single rocker lids	*	*	(from XG42304)
disc front brake		*	

T120R

Feature	'71	'72	'73	
oil-in-frame	*	*	*	
conical hubs	*	*	*	
push-in exhaust pipes		*	*	(from XG42304)
single rocker lids		*	*	(from XG42304)
disc front brake			*	

T120V

Feature	'72	'73	'74	'75	
oil-in-frame	*	*	*	*	
conical hubs	*	*	*	*	
five-speed	*	*	*	*	
push-in exhaust pipes	*	*			(from XG42304)
single rocker lids	*	*			(from XG42304)
disc front brake			*	*	*
reverse cone silencers				*	*

T120RV

Feature	'72	'73	'74	'75	
oil-in-frame	*	*	*	*	
conical hubs	*	*	*	*	
five-speed	*	*	*	*	
push-in exhaust pipes	*	*			(from XG42304)
single rocker lids	*	*			(from XG42304)
disc front brake			*	*	*
reverse cone silencers				*	*

T65

Feature	'73
TR6 model	*
1969 front brake	*
full-width hub	*

Thunderbird 600

Feature	'83
custom style	*
16 in. rear wheel	*
2-level seat	*
drum rear brake	*
wire wheels	*
2-disc opt	*

Daytona 600

Feature	'83
tail fairing	*
drum rear brake	*
2 carburettors	*
wire wheels	*
2-disc opt	*

TR65

Feature	'81	'82
matt-black engine	*	*
single carb	*	*
points ignition	*	*
drum rear brake	*	*
2-1 exhaust	*	
std exhausts		*
2-disc opt		*

TR65T

Feature	'82
21 in. front wheel	*
disc front brake	*
drum rear brake	*
2-1 exhaust	*
matt-black finish	*
undershield	*
electronic ignition	*

TR7RV

Feature	'73	'74	'75
10-stud head	*	*	*
disc front brake	*	*	*
five-speed	*	*	*
reverse cone silencers		*	*

TR7V

Feature	'76	'77	'78	'79	'80	'81
10-stud head	*	*	*	*	*	*
disc front brake	*	*	*	*	*	*
five-speed	*	*	*	*	*	*
rear disc brake	*	*	*	*	*	*
left gear lever	*	*	*	*	*	*
electronic ignition				*	*	*
rear caliper above disc					*	*
clamped exhaust pipes						*
2-1 exhaust opt						*
Morris cast wheels opt						*

TR7T Tiger Trail

Feature	'81	'82
21 in. front wheel	*	*
disc front brake	*	*
drum rear brake	*	*
2-1 exhaust	*	*
matt-black finish	*	*
undershield	*	*

T140V

Feature	Model year					
	'73	'74	'75	'76	'77	'78
2 carbs	*	*	*	*	*	*
10-stud head	*	*	*	*	*	*
disc front brake	*	*	*	*	*	*
five-speed	*	*	*	*	*	*
reverse cone silencers		*	*	*	*	*
rear disc brake				*	*	*
left gear lever				*	*	*

T140RV

Feature	Model year		
	'73	'74	'75
2 carbs	*	*	*
10-stud head	*	*	*
disc front brake	*	*	*
five-speed	*	*	*
reverse cone silencers		*	*

T140 Silver Jubilee

Feature	Model year
	'77
special finish	*

T140D Bonneville Special

Feature	Model year	
	'79	'80
2 carbs	*	*
10-stud head	*	*
disc front brake	*	*
five-speed	*	*
rear disc brake	*	*
left gear lever	*	*
Lester alloy wheels	*	*
2–1 exhaust	*	*
stepped seat	*	*
rear caliper above disc	*	*

T140E

Feature	Model year				
	'78	'79	'80	'81	'82
2 Amal Mk II carbs	*	*	*	*	*
10-stud head	*	*	*	*	*
parallel inlet ports	*	*	*	*	*
disc front brake	*	*	*	*	*
five-speed	*	*	*	*	*
rear disc brake	*	*	*	*	*
left gear lever	*	*	*	*	*
electronic ignition		*	*	*	*
rear caliper above disc			*	*	*
2–1 exhaust opt				*	*
Morris cast wheels opt				*	*
dual front disc opt				*	*
electric start opt				*	*
cockpit fairing opt				*	*

T140ES

Feature	Model year			
	'80	'81	'82	'83
2 Amal Mk II carbs	*	*	*	*
10-stud head	*	*	*	*
parallel inlet ports	*	*	*	*
disc front brake	*	*	*	*
five-speed	*	*	*	*
rear disc brake	*	*	*	*
left gear lever	*	*	*	*
electronic ignition	*	*	*	*
electric start	*	*	*	*
rear caliper above disc	*	*	*	*
2–1 exhaust opt		*	*	*
Morris cast wheels opt		*	*	*
dual front disc opt		*	*	*
tail fairing				*
no kickstart				*

T140 Executive

Feature	Model year		
	'80	'81	'82
As T140ES plus	*	*	*
Sabre cockpit fairing	*	*	*
Sigma panniers and top box	*	*	*
T140ES options		*	*
full-fairing opt		*	*
Bing carburettors		*	*

T140 Royal

Feature	Model year
	'81
As T140ES but	*
Bing carbs	*
USA model—wire wheels and one front disc	*
UK model—Morris wheels and dual disc	*

T140TSS

Feature	Model year	
	'82	'83
8-valve engine	*	*
alloy top half	*	*
Amal carbs	*	*
Marzocchi rear units	*	*
wire wheels	*	*
dual front discs	*	*
cast wheel opt	*	*
antivibration opt		*
no kickstart		*

T140TSX

Feature	Model year	
	'82	'83
custom style	*	*
Bing carbs	*	*
16 in. rear wheel	*	*
alloy wheels	*	*
megaphone silencers	*	*
two-level seat	*	*
dual disc opt	*	*
8-valve engine opt		*
no kickstart		*

Devon twins

Feature	'85	'86	'87	'88
UK and USA builds	*	*	*	*
744 cc five-speed	*	*	*	*
Amal 1½ Concentric carbs	*	*	*	*
wire wheels	*	*	*	*
dual front discs	*	*	*	*
disc rear brake	*	*	*	*

Triples

T150

Feature	'68	'69	'70	'71	'72
vertical cylinders	*	*	*	*	*
ray gun silencers	*	*	*		
megaphone silencer				*	*
tls front brake	*				
bellcrank tls brake		*	*		
conical hubs				*	*
slimline forks				*	*
no rear unit lower cover			*		
no rear unit covers				*	*
turn signals				*	*

T150V

Feature	'72	'73	'74
vertical cylinders	*	*	*
five-speed	*	*	*
megaphone silencer	*	*	*
conical front hub	*		

T150V

Feature	'72	'73	'74
disc front brake		*	*
conical rear hub	*	*	*
slimline forks	*	*	*
no rear unit covers	*	*	*
turn signals	*	*	*
fork gaiters		*	*

T160

Feature	'75	'76
inclined cylinders	*	*
five-speed	*	*
electric start	*	*
disc rear brake	*	*

X75

Feature	'73
custom style	*
inclined cylinders	*
exhausts on right	*
conical hubs	*

Single-cylinder models

T15

Feature	'53	'54	'55	'56
plunger frame	*	*	*	*
gear indicator		*	*	*

T20

Feature	'54	'55	'56	'57	'58	'59	'60	'61	'62	'63	'64	'65	'66
plunger frame	*	*	*										
S/A frame				*	*	*	*	*	*	*	*	*	*
gear indicator	*	*	*	*	*	*	*	*	*				
rod indicator										*	*		
upswept exhaust	*												
coil enclosed			*										
16 in. wheels			*	*	*	*							
17 in. wheels							*	*	*	*	*	*	
18 in. wheels													*
4–bar badge	*	*	*										
grill badge				*	*	*	*	*	*	*	*	*	*
points housing	*	*	*	*	*	*	*	*	*				
timing case points										*	*	*	*
Amal carb	*	*	*	*						*	*	*	*
Zenith carb					*	*	*	*	*				
rear skirt						*	*	*	*	*	*	*	
engine c/l split (from engine 57617)							*	*	*	*	*	*	*
finned rocker cover										*	*	*	*
Bantam D7 frame													*

T20S/C

Feature	'67	'68
Bantam D7 frame	*	*
Bantam D7 tank	*	*
4–bar badge	*	*
full-width hubs	*	*

T20C

Feature	'57	'58	'59
nacelle	*	*	*
19 in. front tyre	*	*	*
upswept exhaust	*	*	*
4–bar badge	*	*	*
undershield	*	*	*
Zenith carb		*	*
extra engine fins			*

T20S

Feature	'60
4–bar badge	*
waist-level exhaust	*
ET ignition	*
direct lights	*
heavy-duty forks	*
19 in. front tyre	*
undershield	*
rev counter	*

T20T

Feature	'61
4–bar badge	*
Zenith carb	*
waist-level exhaust	*
ET ignition	*
direct lights	*
heavy-duty forks	*
19 in. front tyre	*
undershield	*
rev counter opt	*

T20S/L

Feature	'61
4–bar badge	*
waist-level exhaust	*
ET ignition	*
direct lights	*
heavy-duty forks	*
19 in. front tyre	*
undershield	*
rev counter opt	*

T20S/S

Feature	'62	'63	'64	'65	'66
4–bar badge	*	*	*	*	*
Amal carb	*	*	*	*	*
low-level exhaust	*	*	*	*	*

T20S/S

Feature	'62	'63	'64	'65	'66
ET ignition	*	*	*	*	*
direct lights	*	*	*	*	*
heavy-duty forks	*	*	*	*	*
19 in. front tyre	*	*	*	*	*
undershield	*	*	*	*	*
rev counter opt	*	*	*	*	*
points housing	*				
timing cover points			*	*	*
cranked kickstart lever				*	*

T20S/H

Feature	'62	'63	'64	'65	'66
grill badge	*	*	*	*	*
Amal carb	*	*	*	*	*
low-level exhaust	*	*	*	*	*
coil ignition	*	*	*	*	*
switches under seat	*	*	*	*	*
battery box	*	*	*	*	*
heavy-duty forks	*	*	*	*	*
19 in. front tyre	*	*	*	*	*
undershield	*	*			
points housing	*				
timing cover points		*	*	*	*
finned rocker covers		*	*	*	*
cranked kickstart lever				*	*

TR20

Feature	'62	'63	'64	'65	'66
ET ignition	*	*	*	*	*
short seat	*	*	*	*	*
inboard exhaust	*	*	*	*	*
waist-level pipe	*	*	*	*	*
tubular silencer	*	*	*	*	*
heavy-duty forks	*	*	*	*	*
alloy mudguards	*	*	*	*	*
21 in. front wheel	*	*	*	*	*
18 in. rear wheel	*	*	*	*	*
points housing	*				
timing cover points		*	*	*	*
finned rocker covers		*	*	*	*

TS20

Feature	'62	'63	'64
ET ignition	*	*	*
short seat	*	*	*
inboard exhaust	*	*	*
waist-level pipe	*	*	*
open exhaust	*	*	*
heavy-duty forks	*	*	*
alloy mudguards	*	*	*
21 in. front wheel	*	*	*
19 in. rear wheel	*	*	*
points housing	*		
timing cover points		*	*
finned rocker covers		*	*

T20SM Model year

Feature	'65	'66
off-road trail format in yellow	*	*

TR25W Model year

Feature	'68	'69	'70
waist-level exhaust	*	*	*
inboard pipe	*		
outboard pipe		*	*
exhaust on left			*
mesh heat shield		*	*
eyebrow badge	*		
frame badge		*	*
full-width front hub	*	*	*
bellcrank tls brake		*	*
crinkle rear hub	*	*	*
oil-pressure switch			*

T25SS Model year

Feature	'71
oil-in-frame	*
slimline forks	*
conical hubs	*
tls front brake	*
18 in. front wheel	*
unsprung front guard	*

T25T Model year

Feature	'71
oil-in-frame	*
slimline forks	*
conical hubs	*
20 in. front wheel	*
sprung front guard	*

TR5MX Model year

Feature	'73	'74
oil-in-frame	*	*
conical hubs	*	*
21 in. front wheel	*	*
twin silencers	*	*

Hinckley models

Model	'91	'92	'93	'94	'95	'96	'97
Trident 750	*	*	*	*	*	*	*
Trident 900	*	*	*	*	*	*	*
Sprint 900			*	*	*	*	*
Trophy 900	*	*	*	*	*	*	*
Trophy 1200	*	*	*	*	*	*	
Daytona 750	*	*					
Daytona 1000	*	*					
Daytona 900			*	*	*	*	
Daytona 1200			*	*	*	*	*
Tiger 900			*	*	*	*	*
Speed Triple 900			*	*	*		
Daytona Super III			*	*	*		
Thunderbird					*	*	*
Adventurer						*	*
T509 Speed Triple							*
T595 Daytona							*

Colours

The following colour charts are included to aid in identifying model years and types and are thus in outline form rather than in full detail as in *Triumph Twin Restoration*. Most of the detail parts on the machines will be in black while the wheel rims may be black, chrome plated with painted centres or simply chrome plated. Headlamp shells may be painted or plated, and some mudguards were in light alloy or stainless steel. The data should assist you when viewing a machine, since an incorrect colour indicates either a change of part or a repaint. This may not matter to you but it is good to know.

Prewar singles and Page twin

6/1

1934–36   All-black, tank chrome with black panels

Tiger models

1936   Black, tank chrome with silver sheen panels and chrome rims

1937–38   Black, silver mudguard ribs, tank chrome with silver sheen panels, chrome rims and headlamp

1939–40   Black, silver mudguards with black ribs, tank chrome with silver sheen panels, chrome rims and headlamp

De Luxe

1937   Black, tank chrome with plum panels

1938   Black, tank chrome with deep-red panels

1939–40   Black, tank chrome with black panels

Std 3SE, 5SE

1940   All-black

Pre-unit twins

3T

1946–49   Black, tank chrome with ivory panels

1950-51   All-black

5T

1938–49   All-Amaranth Red, tank chrome with red panels

1950–56   All-Amaranth Red

1957–58   Amaranth Red tank and mudguards

6T

1950   All-blue-grey

1951–55   All-polychromatic blue

1956   All-crystal grey

1957–58   Bronze-gold tank and mudguards

1959   Charcoal-grey tank and mudguards

1960   As 1959, with charcoal-grey for bath-tub

1961–62   Silver lower tank, front mudguard and bathtub

T100

1939–49   Silver mudguards, tank chrome with silver panels

1950–53   Silver tank and mudguards

1954–56   Shell blue tank and mudguards

1957   Silver-grey tank and mudguards, option of tank with ivory top and blue lower plus ivory mudguards

1958   Standard as 1957, option of tank with black top and ivory lower and mudguards

1959   Standard as 1957, option of tank with black lower and ivory top and mudguards

T110

1954–56   Shell blue tank and mudguards

1957   Silver-grey tank and mudguards, option of tank with ivory top and blue lower plus ivory mudguards

166

T110

1958	Standard as 1957, option of tank with black top and ivory lower and mudguards
1959	Standard as 1957, option of tank with black lower and ivory top and mudguards
1960	All-black, with ivory tank lower
1961	Kingfisher blue tank top, fork upper legs and nacelle, silver lower, front mudguard and bathtub

T120

1959–60	Pearl-grey tank top and mudguards, tangerine lower; during first year changed to pearl-grey tank top, mudguards, oil tank and toolbox with royal blue tank lower
1961	Sky blue tank top and silver lower, mudguards, oil tank and battery box
1962	Sky blue tank top, silver lower and mudguards

TR5

1949–54	Silver mudguards, tank chrome with silver panels
1955–56	Shell blue tank and mudguards
1957–58	Silver-grey tank and mudguards

TR6

1956	Shell blue tank and mudguards
1957–58	Silver-grey tank and mudguards
1959	Standard as 1957, export option with tank top in ivory and lower in Aztec red
1960	Ivory tank top and mudguards with Aztec red lower
1961	Ruby red tank top, silver lower and mudguards
1962	Polychromatic burgundy tank top, silver lower and mudguards

Unit twins

3TA

1957–62	Shell blue tank, forks, front mudguard and bathtub
1963	Standard as 1957, option of silver-bronze for shell blue parts
1964	Silver-bronze tank, forks, mudguards and skirt
1965	As 1964, in silver-beige
1966	Pacific blue tank top, Alaskan white lower and mudguards

5TA

1959	All-Amaranth Red
1960–62	All-ruby red
1963	All-cherry red
1964–65	Silver tank lower, mudguards and skirt
1966	Silver tank lower and mudguards

T90

1963	Alaskan white tank, mudguards and rear skirt
1964	Gold tank top, Alaskan white lower and mudguards
1965	Pacific blue tank top, silver lower and mudguards
1966	Grenadier red tank top, Alaskan white lower and mudguards
1967	Hi-fi scarlet tank top, Alaskan white lower and mudguards
1968	Riviera blue tank top, silver lower and mudguards

T100A

1960	All-black, with ivory tank lower
1961	Silver tank lower, front mudguard and bathtub

T100SS

1962	Kingfisher blue tank top and skirt, silver lower and mudguards
1963	Regal purple tank top and skirt, silver lower and mudguards
1964	Scarlet tank top, silver lower and mudguards
1965	Burnished gold tank top, Alaskan white lower and mudguards

T100

1966	Sherbourne green tank top, Alaskan white lower and mudguards
1967	Pacific blue tank top, Alaskan white lower and mudguards
1968	Aquamarine-green tank top, silver lower and mudguards
1969	Lincoln green tank top, silver lower and mudguards
1970	Jacaranda purple tank top, silver lower and mudguards; T100S with all-silver tank
1971	Olympic flame tank and mudguards
1972	Cherry tank and mudguards
1973	Hi-fi vermilion and ice white tank
1974	Argosy blue and ice white tank

TR5T

1973–74	All-black, with alloy tank with yellow side panels; sometimes red panels

6T

1963–65	Black tank top, silver lower, front mudguard and skirt
1966	Black tank top, silver lower and mudguards

TR6

1963	Regal purple tank top, silver lower and mudguards
1964	Hi-fi scarlet tank top, silver lower and mudguards
1965	Burnished gold tank top and Alaskan white lower

TR6
1966	Pacific blue tank top, Alaskan white lower and mudguards
1967	Mist green tank top, Alaskan white lower and mudguards
1968	Riviera blue tank top, silver lower and mudguards
1969	Trophy red tank top, silver lower and mudguards
1970	Spring gold tank and mudguards
1971	Pacific blue and white tank and blue mudguards
1972–73	Polychromatic blue tank top and mudguards, white lower

T120
1963	Alaskan white tank and mudguards
1964	Gold tank top, Alaskan white lower and mudguards
1965	Pacific blue tank top, silver lower and mudguards
1966	Grenadier red tank top, Alaskan white lower and mudguards
1967	Aubergine (purple) tank top, Alaskan white lower and mudguards
1968	Hi-fi scarlet tank top, silver lower and mudguards
1969	Olympic flame tank top, silver lower and mudguards
1970	Astral red tank with silver side panels, red mudguards
1971	Tiger gold with black tank, gold mudguards
1972	Tiger gold tank top and mudguards, white lower
1973	Hi-fi vermilion and gold tank
1974–75	Purple and white tank

TR7
1973	Astral blue and opal tank
1974–77	Jade green and white tank
1978	Brown and gold or aquamarine and silver for tank and mudguards
1979	Black and candy apple red or brown and gold or aquamarine and silver for tank and side panels
1980–81	Red, blue, black, black and red, gold and red or silver and blue in various styles for tank and side covers

TR7T
| 1981–82 | Yellow tank, side covers and mudguards with black engine and exhaust system |

TR65T
| 1982 | As TR7T |

T140
| 1973 | Hi-fi vermilion and gold tank |
| 1974–75 | Cherokee red and white tank |

T140
| 1976–77 | Polychromatic red or blue tank with white side panels |
| 1978 | Brown and gold or aquamarine and silver for tank and mudguards |

Jubilee
| 1977 | Special red, white and blue finish with lots of chrome and polish |

T140E
1978	Black and candy apple red tank
1979	Black and candy apple red or brown and gold or aquamarine and silver for tank and side panels
1980–81	Red, blue, black, black and red, gold and red or silver and blue in various styles for tank and side covers
1982	Black and red tank
1983	Black or black with stripes on tank and side covers

T140D
| 1979–80 | All-black |

Executive
| 1980–82 | Deep maroon shading to ruby |

Royal
| 1981 | Special finish |

TSS
| 1982 | All-black |
| 1983 | Black and red tank |

TSX
| 1982 | Red tank and side covers |
| 1983 | Red or black tank and side covers with stripes |

TR65
| 1981 | Smokey cherry red or regal purple |
| 1982 | Smokey cherry red or blue and silver |

Thunderbird 600
| 1983 | All-black, with stripes on tank and side covers |

Daytona 600
| 1983 | Red tank, side covers and tail fairing |

Devon twins
| 1985–88 | Black or black and red tank |

Triples
T150
1968–69	Aquamarine tank and mudguards
1970	Orange mudguards and tank with white panels
1971	Black with white tank panels
1972	Regal purple tank and side covers
1973	Black and red tank
1974	Black and gold tank

T160
| 1975–76 | Cherokee red with white panels or white with yellow panels for tank |

X75
| 1973 | Red tank, side panel and seat base moulding with yellow stripes |

Singles

T15

1953–56   All-Amaranth Red

T20

1954–56   Shell blue tank and mudguards

1957–58   Silver-grey tank and mudguards

1959–60   Silver-grey tank, oil tank, toolbox, mudguards and skirt

1961   Black tank top, silver sheen lower, oil tank, toolbox, mudguards and skirt

1962   Flame tank top, silver-grey lower, oil tank, toolbox, mudguards and skirt

1963   Flame tank top, oil tank and toolbox lid with tank lower, mudguards and skirt in silver-grey

1964–65   Hi-fi scarlet tank top, oil tank and toolbox lid with tank lower, mudguards and skirt in silver-grey

1966   Pacific blue tank top, oil tank, battery cover and toolbox lid with Alaskan white tank lower and mudguards

T20S/C

1967–68   Bushfire red tank, mudguards, oil tank, centre panels and toolbox lid with chrome on tank side

T20C

1957–59   Silver-grey tank and mudguards

T20S

1960   Silver-grey tank and mudguards

T20T

1961   Ruby red tank top, silver lower and mudguards

T20S/L

1961   Ruby red tank top, silver lower and mudguards

T20S/S

1962–66   Burgundy tank top, silver lower and mudguards

T20S/H

1962–63   Burgundy tank top, silver-grey lower and mudguards

1964–65   Hi-fi scarlet tank top, silver-grey lower and mudguards

T20S/H

1966   Pacific blue tank top, oil tank, battery cover and toolbox lid with Alaskan white tank lower and mudguards

TR20

1962–63   Burgundy tank top, silver-grey lower, alloy mudguards

1964–66   Hi-fi scarlet tank top, silver-grey lower, alloy mudguards

TS20

1962–63   Burgundy tank top, silver-grey lower, alloy mudguards

1964   Hi-fi scarlet tank top, silver-grey lower, alloy mudguards

T20SM

1965–66   Finished in yellow

TR25W

1968   Flamboyant red tank

1969–70   Hi-fi scarlet tank

T25SS

1971   Tank coloured with flash

T25T

1971   Tank coloured with flash

Scooters

All

1959–60   Shell blue sheen

1961   Shell blue sheen, options in primrose or grey or in any colour with ivory apron

1962–65   Shell blue sheen, options in mimosa or grey or in any colour with ivory apron

Tina

1962–65   Lilac

T10

1965–66   Flamboyant red

1967   Translucent ruby or ruby Amaranth with options in mimosa and ivory or blue and ivory

1968–70   Flamboyant red

Hinckley

From the start the machines were available in a choice of colors and these varied from year to year. A two-tone finish was used for some, engines could be natural, black or with polished covers, and there was variation in the detail fittings as well as the frame, forks and wheels. For these modern machines, reference to the applicable brochure will give the detailed information.

Clubs, spares and manuals

An important aspect of motorcycling is knowing where to get parts and information for your machine. Spares and services are essential to all owners at some time or other, and a list of people and firms who can help can be useful at times of stress. The owners club can help with this and is well worth joining, regardless of where you live. It will provide addresses and contacts which can be just what is needed at times.

To locate the club and dealers use one or more of the current motorcycle magazines. Browse through publications at your local newsstand, bookstore or public library for titles such as the weekly *Motor Cycle News*, although for a Triumph you are likely to be better off with magazines such as *Classic Bike, Classic Motor Cycle, Classic Mechanics, Old Bike Mart* or *British Bike Magazine*. Within their pages you will find the contact address for the Triumph Owner's Club, and advertisements for services and parts. I have not included club and publication names and addresses here due to their highly changeable nature.

As an enthusiast, you need to keep abreast of the market changes, especially on the matter of prices which are also not included here, since they are outdated even faster than club secretaries. You should be using the ads to check out values and asking prices well before you go out to shop. This is the way to get good value. Make full use of the magazines in this way as well as for tracking down things you need.

Data Sources

Your sources are the books, parts lists and manuals. The Triumph owner is fortunate in having an ample supply of literature available, which does make ownership easier.

Haynes and Clymer manuals cover many of the Triumph models in their own special ways. They are useful, but make sure that the one you use is relevant to your model.

Factory manuals and parts lists, which are the official word but no longer available other than in reprint now. Copies of the genuine Triumph books can be found at autojumbles and swap meets, but some years are harder to find than others. Basically there was one parts list for each model year, and it will have the starting engine number on the cover. This generally applies but not always, and there are some lists that either cover more than one year or have supplements that go with them for a year or two or for additional models. Thus the list for the 1960 twins of 650 cc has supplements for 1961 and 1962, while one of the Cub lists has a two-page leaflet to cover the TR20 and TS20. In the 1970s the firm tended to produce a USA parts list and a supplement to show the changes for the home and general export markets. Photocopies of most manuals and lists can be obtained, as can reproductions of the later material. For both, follow the advertisements in the magazines and you will soon locate what you need.

Triumph Twins & Triples by Roy Bacon, reprinted by Niton

A history of the twins and triples that concentrates on the Turner designs but includes the earlier models. It includes information on the military machines, scooter twin, specials and the use of the machines in competition. The detailed appendices are a strong feature and include specifications, engine and frame numbers, colours, recognition points, model chart and carburettor settings.

Triumph Twin Restoration by Roy Bacon, published by Osprey

A guide for restoration and parts identification which thus includes the development history of the Turner twins from 1938 to 1972. The very extensive appendices have been highly praised by reviewers and this is the book you need to turn a basket job into a concours winner.

Triumph Singles by Roy Bacon, reprinted by Niton

A history that majors on the Terrier and Cub models but which starts at the earliest models with a brief summary up to the 1930s and then more detail on that period. Includes chapters on the Tigress and Tina scooters, the BSA clones and the single in competition from that 1908 TT win. Has the same detailed appendices as the twins and triples book. Second edition has more information on colour for UK and USA models.

Triumph Bonneville T120, 1959-1974 by Roy Bacon, published by Niton in Monograph series

Small format booklet detailing the history of this model in its various forms from start to finish. Well illustrated with over 50 pictures.

Triumph Tiger 100 & 110, 1939-1961 by Roy Bacon, published by Niton in Monograph series

The sports twin which followed the launch of the Speed Twin and continued postwar together with the larger version, both very popular. Well illustrated with over 50 contemporary pictures.

Triumph T140 Bonneville & Derivatives, 1973-1988 by Roy Bacon, published by Niton in Monograph series

Continues the Bonneville story in its larger capacity form and includes the models derived from it in the final days of the Meriden twin. Well pictured as usual in the series.

Triumph Touring Twins, 3T-5T-6T-3TA-5TA, 1938-1966 by Roy Bacon, published by Niton in Monograph series

The Speed Twin started the change to the vertical twin and tourers remained in the range for many years. Amply illustrated.

Triumph T90 & T100 Unit Twins, 1960-1974 by Roy Bacon, published by Niton in Monograph series

The smaller unit twins had their own style and enthusiastic buyers. This book charts their progress and is well pictured.

BSA Rocket 3 & Triumph Trident, 1968-1976 by Roy Bacon, published by Niton in Monograph series

The triples with either badge were closely associated, although the Trident was the more popular with the customers. Well illustrated.

The Story of Triumph Motorcycles by Harry Louis and Bob Currie, published by Patrick Stephens

A full marque history presented in a somewhat confusing chapter order rather than as a chronological story. Written more in the style of a series of feature articles than as a book but covers the history fully.

It's a Triumph by Ivor Davies, published by Haynes

The Triumph story, as seen by the advertising manager of the firm in its postwar years, with a very extensive number of photographs from the earliest days. Not a history as such but full of stories of the men and machines from Meriden.

Pictorial History of Triumph Motor Cycles by Ivor Davies, published by Temple Press

A photo history with lengthy captions to the pictures but minimal text otherwise.

Its easy on a Triumph by Ivor Davies, published by Haynes

Photos and anecdotes of Triumphs and the men who built and rode them. A good insight into 'behind the scenes' at the factory and elsewhere.

Triumph Twins from 1937 compiled by Cyril Ayton, published by Bay View Books

Reprints of road tests and articles on the twins from 1937 to 1966.

Triumph by Don Morley, published by Osprey in their Classic Motorcycles series

An all-colour photo book with pictures to the usual high standard associated with the Morley name and camera.

Triumph: The Complete Story by Ivor Davies, published by Crowood

A good history with some personal reminiscences.

Bonnie by John Nelson, published by Haynes

Highly detailed development history of the Bonneville from its start in 1959 right through to 1978 with year by year changes, specifications, colours and photographs. If you have a T120 then you need this book.

Tiger 100 by John Nelson, published by Haynes

On the same lines as Bonnie and equally suitable if you have a T100. Covers all the models.

Tiger 100/Daytona by John Nelson, published by J.R.Technical Publications

Companion to Tiger 100 with detailed specifications and part numbers on year by year basis.

Speed Twin by Harry Woolridge, published by Haynes

Covers the touring twins on the lines of Bonnie and Tiger 100 so essential for the fine detail.

The First Classic Triumph Scene by Bruce Main-Smith

Written by, photographed for and published by B. M-S. in his Scene book series

with some 125 pictures in 64 pages, all taken of machines as they are now and all but three of postwar models. Useful reference material.

Triumph Tuning by Stan Shenton

Detailed information on both twins and triples by the man who ran the very successful Boyer team of production racers in the 1960s and 1970s. Highly recommended for real performance with reliability information and full of detail points that make the difference between a finish or a retirement.

Meriden Historical Summary 1972-74 published by NVT

History of the firm before, during and after the famous sit-in at Meriden. Small booklet, no pictures, just history.

Triumph Bonneville Super Profile by John Nelson, published by Haynes

Brief history of the one model in usual format for this series with details of development and competition use plus a photo gallery in colour as well as black and white.

Triumph Thunderbird Super Profile by Ivor Davies, published by Haynes

Brief history as above with good range of colour brochure pictures for most years this popular model was produced.

Triumph Trident Super Profile by Ivor Davies, published by Haynes

Brief history of the much loved triple in the same format as above.

Triumph Motor Cycles by A.St.J.Masters, published by Pearson

Long out of print but one in a series written by the service managers of the firms and bound in red covers. Very good coverage from 1937 on and still to be found in various editions at autojumbles.

Triumph Twin Motor Cycles by A.St.J.Masters, published by Pearson

Another of the little red books with data from 1945 on into the 1960s.

Triumph Motor Cycles (single cylinder) by A.St.J.Masters, published by Pearson

This one deals with the prewar models built from 1937, the military 3HW and the Terrier and Cub ranges in various editions up to the 1960s.

The Book of the Triumph Twins by W.C.Haycroft, published by Pitman

Many editions produced into the 1970s but not so deep or as highly regarded as the Pearson series. For all that, a handy publication to have on the shelf.

The Book of the BSA Sunbeam and Triumph Tigress Motor Scooters by John Thorpe, published by Pitman

Useful cover of both twin- and single-cylinder models of either marque in usual format of this series.

Triumph: The Illustrated Motorcycle Legends by Roy Bacon, published by Sunburst.

A large-format pictorial history using factory brochure material and photographs, mainly in color.

Triumph Motorcycles in America by Lindsay Brooke and David Gaylin, published by Motorbooks International. An in-depth study of the Triumph USA scene from its earliest days. It brings to light much that has not been previously recorded and offers a wealth of information on the machines and men who operated in the USA.

Triumph Racing Motorcycles in America by Lindsay Brooke, published by Motorbooks International.

Companion volume to the above covering the competition history in the United States.

Triumph: The Return of the Legend by Dave Minton.

A marque history from the pen of a well-known journalist that includes the Hinckley events and is illustrated with color and b/w photographs.

Tales of Triumph by Hughie Hancox, published by Veloce.

Stories of the Meriden days from an employee who worked there for 20 years and has since become a top restorer, specializing in Triumph twins.

The Daytona T595 supersport model was new for 1997 with a larger triple engine, fuel injection, and a new chassis.

Index